To Veronica w. ♡

reliability makes
miracles happen!

Miracles Relied Upon

Happy 2013!

Genny

Miracles Relied Upon

A History of the
People's Resource Center

Margaret and Warren Roth

Copyright © 2012 Margaret and Warren Roth

All rights reserved. No part of this book may be reproduced or transmitted in any form or by any means, electronic or mechanical, including photo-copying, recording or by any information and retrieval system without permission from the authors and the People's Resource Center.

Editing and composition: WorldViews/Thomas P. Fenton
Cover design: KDesign (www.kantorskidesign.com)/Joseph Kantorski
Proofreading: Mary J. Heffron

ISBN-13: 978-1478302230
ISBN-10: 1478302232

Contents

Mission Statement

People's Resource Center community exists to respond to basic human needs, promote dignity and justice, and create a future of hope and opportunity for the residents of DuPage County, Illinois, through discovering and sharing personal and community resources.

Values

Dignity and Respect
We recognize the dignity of each person who comes to us, and we create a welcoming and respectful environment in all of our programs and communication.

Creative and Innovative
We express our mission directly. We try things in the community. We are willing to jump in to new areas in order to address an unmet need.

Responsible Stewards
We welcome those who need resources, as well as those with resources to share.

Compassionate
We listen, we encourage, we try to get to know our families; we promote some help and guidance; we advocate, in a spirit of kindness and compassion.

Integrity
We place a high priority in living out our principles, in our relationships, programs, and organizational practices.

...And We Rely on Miracles!!
We know that we cannot do it alone. We rely on each other, on our friends in the community, and on God, who brings us all together.

Introduction

THE COMMUNITY THAT IS THE PEOPLE'S RESOURCE CENTER can trace its origins to 1965. A chance meeting between two like-minded residents of DuPage County, Illinois, led to an evolutionary process that today brings hope and a measure of stability to the lives of more than three thousand people each month.

Through the remainder of the 1960s and 1970s, a period of social unrest, three distinct centers came into existence, and morphed into each other to become known to the residents of DuPage County as the People's Resource Center. The first of these centers was the Religious Education Center (REC), which had its humble beginnings in 1966. By 1974, REC had given birth to the Peace and Justice Center and it, in turn, brought forth the PRC in 1975. The common designation of "center" for each organization was no accident. Each was meant to draw people together for their own good and for the good of the larger society in which they lived.

REC has since changed its name to the Religious Education Community because its members came to realize that only in the strong bonds of community could they accomplish its active mission. REC remains in existence and its members strive to keep the community spirit in the PRC even as the offspring organization grows and becomes a well organized and effective force for good in DuPage County. The goals of the Peace and

Justice Center are also being carried out by the combined efforts of a number of peace groups in the county.

The account that follows is a summary of the combined recollections of those who have been involved in any or all three organizations. There are some written records of the earliest days, but the Centers were more about action than archives. Oral history is, therefore, the main source from which this book is drawn. The authors recognize that there may be memories of the early days, especially of those who were involved in that time, that do not fit the descriptions in the following text. We apologize for any factual errors and ask pardon of anyone who might be offended by them. Our aim has been to get as much oral history into print as possible before the history makers have gone from our midst. Perhaps future writers will take up the challenge of updating and revising what we have written.

Preface

About the Title

"Miracles Relied Upon" comes from Dorothy McIntyre's account of an event during the early days of the People's Resource Center. She told of an afternoon when the food on the pantry shelves was almost all gone. PRC's finances were at one of their low points and a food distribution day was coming up. A truck pulled up in front of the PRC's rented house and the driver came in and announced that he had five or six pallets of canned goods from a church food drive. In recounting the story, Dorothy uttered the words that have become a mantra for those working at the PRC: "I don't believe in miracles, I rely on them."

There would be other instances, some recorded in this book, when "miracles" happened just when they were most needed. It therefore seemed appropriate to title this history of the PRC with a paraphrase of Dorothy's words.

Names Mentioned

The reader of this history will come across names of many persons who have played important roles in the growth and development of the PRC. It should be expected that an organization whose name begins with "People's" would record the names of many of them. For the authors, identifying these people was necessary because in their own ways, each helped make the PRC what it is today. At the same time, the authors recognize that many who have given much are not mentioned. Just listing all of the present volunteers, over 1,300, would have made the book look more like a telephone directory or a biographical dictionary. We ask forgiveness for the omissions and apologize to those readers who do not find their own names or the names of relatives or friends who gave of themselves so generously in the work of the PRC. Frequent references to REC members is meant to indicate how a small group of community-oriented people can bring about change by their continuous support.

About the Authors

Margaret and Warren Roth suggested writing this history to the PRC board of directors and Executive Director Kim Perez in September 2011. Warren was retiring from the board after eighteen years and he proposed that he and Margaret be designated as a task force to record the history because they had both been involved since the PRC's founding.

Margaret Roth was born in Stuttgart, Germany, and came to the United States in 1968 to teach economics at Rosary College (now Dominican University) in River Forest, Illinois. On the day after she arrived, she was introduced to the Religious Education Center, the forerunner of the People's Resource Center. As the PRC evolved, she became its first treasurer and a volunteer in its early activities. After thirty years of teaching international economics and business at Benedictine University in Lisle, Illinois, she is now professor emerita.

Warren Roth was born in Jersey City, New Jersey. He came to DuPage County in 1949 as a student. Later, as an anthropology professor, he taught at Maryknoll College in Glen Ellyn, Illinois, and at Chicago State University. He has worked as a volunteer and as a board member at the PRC. He is now retired from teaching and from the board of the PRC.

Thanks

The authors owe a great deal to many people in the writing of this history.

PRC Executive Director Kim Perez and the board of directors of the People's Resource Center gave their OK to the project.

Members of the Religious Education Community provided personal recollections of the early days of the PRC as well as of the development of a number of its programs. They also read the manuscript and filled in numerous details of how the PRC came to be and how it grew. These REC members include Nancy Castle, Rosie Dixon, Frank and Kay Goetz, Fran Holtzman, Paul and Eileen LeFort, Dick Nogaj, Ruth Riha, Bob Russo, and Connie Gardner Sunderhaus.

Kim Perez and Barbara Tartaglione, current president of the board, both read the manuscript and gave important suggestions. Mary Ellen Durbin, former executive director, filled in details of her tenure at the PRC. Lyn Conway, former president of the board of directors, provided valuable information on the administration of the organization.

Staff members Linda Cheatham, Melissa Travis, Maryanna Milton, Pam Knight, Lesley Gena, John Victor, Dennis McCann, Al White, and Hank Anzelone, and long-time volunteer Roger Libman contributed information both orally and in writing on the programs they started and continue to develop at the PRC. Lisa Doyle and Jennifer Williamson shared important data on present-day volunteers and partnering initiatives by the PRC.

1

Roots of the People's Resource Center

Religious Education Center

IT WAS LATE SUMMER OF 1965. Two people, coming from very different backgrounds, met for the first time at a large gathering of religion teachers in Aurora, Illinois. One was Maryknoll Father Tom Peyton, director of the Religious Education Institute at Maryknoll College in Glen Ellyn, a few miles to the east in DuPage County. He joined a group discussing the religious education of children in another DuPage town, Downers Grove. Dorothy McIntyre was expressing her views with some frustration because she could not implement the ideas she had about teaching children fundamental religious beliefs. Tom can't recall the details of the conversation between Dorothy and himself, but he does remember clearly the high point of the exchange. In a letter written in 2010, he recounted what happened: "At one point, Dorothy challenged me and said, 'Well, you talk a good game, but can you do what you say.' Of course, I said, 'Sure, give me a chance'."

Health problems prevented Tom from meeting again with Dorothy until January of 1966, when she came to the seminary with Janet Foy, a friend who was also a religion teacher. Dorothy and Janet worked out a plan that led to the meeting of seven couples with Tom at the end of January. The seven couples con-

Fr. Tom Peyton, M.M.,   Dorothy McIntyre,
REC founder   PRC founder

tinued to meet and put together what was to materialize into the
Religious Education Center, which was, in less than a decade, to
give rise to the People's Resource Center. Without realizing it, these
seven couples were following a formula that has guided the PRC to
this day: "If you see a problem, you are anointed to address it."

The problem that initially brought these "founders" together re-
volved around the religious instruction of their children. Catholics
whose children were going to public schools had concerns about
the quality of religious instruction their children were receiving
weekly in their parishes. Almost all the parents had Catholic college backgrounds and were aware of the changes the recently
concluded Second Vatican Council had introduced into the Roman
Catholic Church. The innovation that interested them most was
the new emphasis on more effective participation of the laity in
Church life. For all of them this was a major theme that they
wanted introduced into the religious instruction of their children.
Those in the group who were teaching these religion classes in
their churches had wanted to modify the syllabus and teach the
new ideas of the Council. Their attempts, however, had been
fruitless. They were told that the syllabus had to be taught as
given with no alterations. It was at this point that Tom met with
the seven couples.

Dorothy McIntyre became the unofficial spokesperson of the group. When her attempts to get the syllabus changed in her parish proved unsuccessful, she withdrew her children from the classes. When the REC group asked Tom, as a priest, to use his influence in the syllabus dispute, he declined, saying he could not interfere in a parish matter. He offered an alternative, however: he invited members of the group to attend Maryknoll College's Institute for Religious Education. In the Institute's classroom setting, he explained, they could discuss and then try to implement the kind of changes they were seeking.

While some of the group became involved in Institute sessions, Tom suggested that the whole group begin coming to Maryknoll College to meet. These meetings were Sunday liturgies that allowed all present to respond and comment. The liturgies soon became ecumenical. The original group expanded in size as word began to spread that the religious instruction problem was being addressed. The group had already named itself the Religious Education Center and was putting out a bulletin. After a few liturgy meetings at Maryknoll, the members compiled an address list with the names, addresses, and telephone numbers of twenty-five families. As the families got to know each other, Tom began to talk about "community" at their meetings, and as the dialogue went on with him and with each other, some of the participants started using "REC" to designate the group and calling it the REC community. For those who were already in action-oriented organizations, like peace groups, forming committees of REC members was the obvious next step. In the committees that met in homes, social problems and possible solutions were brought up and the results of the committee meetings were presented to the large group on Sundays.

Two of the committees that met regularly were listed in the bulletins as Social Action and Education. These committees grew as REC membership increased. Discussions became spirited and at times heated as the big issue of the day, the Vietnam War, was discussed. Finally, Tom suggested that Social Action discussion be separated from the issue of religious education of children and that it be handled in special sessions. Since REC had no membership requirements, interested people dropped in on home meetings and some added their names to the address list. Fran Holtzman wrote of this period:

> In the late 60's Tom Peyton, knowing I was very concerned
> about the Vietnam War, asked me if I would be interested in
> having some meetings at my home for other interested peo-
> ple. I agreed and every Tuesday we would gather to discuss
> what actions we might take.... It was interesting to open my
> door on Tuesday evening and there were individuals I never
> knew before but they heard about us and wanted to become
> part of the action.

These and many other meetings attracted people with a wide variety of interests and this forced REC members to choose which
social problems they wanted to involve themselves in. This became a stressful time for the group because almost all members
had families and the demands on their time were significantly increased by their commitment to addressing social problems.

Discovering Poverty
in DuPage County

REC's social action became local because of a problem uncovered
by another professor at Maryknoll College. Father Ralph Dávila,
who was bilingual, had been working with Spanish-speaking employees at a food processing plant in West Chicago. There, he
found low wages and poor working conditions to be serious problems. But as he talked to workers and visited their homes he also
discovered that a large group of DuPage County residents were living in poverty. He communicated his finding to other Maryknoll
College faculty and to friends Katherine Fraher and Bob and Ellen
Heelan, who also happened to be REC members. Katherine was in
contact with a large Spanish-speaking family outside of DuPage
County for whom she had enlisted Dávila's help. She began asking
her fellow REC members to contribute clothing and used furniture
for that family. Because of these four people, some of the social action meetings focused on problems close to home. The myth of
affluence for all DuPage County residents was shattering in the
late 1960s, and the seeds of the People's Resource Center were being planted.

Another example of poverty, although not in DuPage County,
came to the attention of REC members at the end of 1967. The bul-

letin contained a note, "thanks to everyone," for the gifts that had been donated to three families in the Robert Taylor public housing apartments in Chicago. Dorothy had befriended a family whose apartment in the same housing complex had been burned out. In the process of helping that family, the needs of three other families came to her attention and she brought these needs to a REC meeting. Money, clothing, and furniture were collected and delivered before Christmas.

Dorothy's contact with the first family continued and REC once again responded to a need. The mother of this first family had been falsely accused of a serious crime in Chicago and was being held in Cook County jail. Dorothy brought the problem to REC and again the response was immediate. Money was collected for bail and a pro bono lawyer was recruited with the help of Bill Sullivan, a REC member whose brother was a prominent attorney in Chicago. When the case came to trial, the judge threw it out for lack of evidence and REC celebrated a social action success.

A little more than a year after that first meeting in Downers Grove, REC had evolved into a community that was ready to address problems beyond the religious education issue that had brought the first group together. The axiom of being "anointed to address a problem you see" was taken seriously and when a need came before the group, REC members took action. In the Easter Sunday *REC Bulletin* in 1968, Tom Peyton included a short note of thanks "to everyone for their generous and prompt response to the clothing and food needs that were communicated on the phone network."

The telephone network had become a rapid response mechanism when needs became known between regular meetings.

Tom explicitly made the case for REC to address the needs of the poor in June of 1968 by providing a practical application for REC members.

> Poverty and oppression exist within the influence of REC and if we do not attack it then REC cannot survive as an authentic Christian community. Our efforts …must rest upon the development of our community through its going out to the needs of all those around us—especially the poor.

He then gave a very specific example of "going out to the poor." In the July 1 edition of *REC Bulletin*, he reported a visit to St. Thomas of Canterbury parish in the Uptown neighborhood of Chicago. He and Dorothy talked to the pastor about the needs of the various ethnic groups in the parish, Native Americans, Appalachian Whites, African Americans, and "the largest concentration of elderly persons in the U.S." He asked REC members who were interested in providing services, from "teaching to plumbing," to form a team and contact Dorothy.

Later in the summer, Fran Holtzman organized a group of REC members for an event to be held at the Church of the Brethren in Lombard. Mike Chosa, a leader of the Native American movement in the Chicago area, was going to make a presentation there and "explain the Indian position." This presentation, which focused on discrimination against Native Americans, led to another social action in Chicago. A group of REC members went to Chicago and tested the housing market. Each would answer an ad for an apartment rental. In all cases, the person from REC was told that the apartment was available for immediate occupancy. A Native American would then inquire about the same apartment and would be told it was not available. This discrimination was one of the issues that Mike Chosa included in the "Indian position."

As 1968 ended, REC had begun to understand the implications of "community" that Peyton was advocating. Its members realized that as individuals they could not have accomplished what they were doing. In the REC community they had like-minded people to call upon when the needs of others were beyond their personal means. The November 24 edition of *REC Bulletin* included thanks to those who came to the aid of a needy family, and Katherine Fraher renewed her requests for the continuing needs of the family she was helping to support. Their fourteen children were well beyond her means.

The importance of the women who joined REC cannot be overstated and their involvement foreshadowed what women would do later in the People's Resource Center. Many of the women in REC were already involved in organizations that were social-action oriented: YWCA, League of Women Voters, and OWL (Older Women's League). The discussion that was going on in the late1960s about a proposed Equal Rights Amendment to the U.S. Constitution had stimulated interest not only in rights but in the problems that people, especially women, faced in society. Those problems were going to be the first focus of the PRC ten years later.

As early as the beginning of 1969, however, Dorothy and Tom were pursuing information about legal status and funding for a family shelter. The idea of a safe house for battered women had come up in meetings as REC members became more involved with families throughout DuPage County. The Family Shelter was the first of a series of initiatives that would begin to expand the scope of REC activities into an organized approach to local social problems. Dorothy and Tom had met with county board members and made their views about voluntary service and public aid known to them. The Family Shelter venture was not something that the board members wanted to hear because they were in denial about social problems in DuPage County. This meant that REC would have to provide the resources for such an innovation. REC members started small by sheltering abused women and children in their homes and turning a two car garage into temporary living quarters, thus gradually building up what was to become the Family Shelter Service.

Growing Pains

The new social action thrust of the REC community was not without its own problems. The number of meetings that were being scheduled and the demands on time that actions entailed were creating a conflict for some REC members who felt that they had to choose between social action and their work and family obligations. One member, a dentist, expressed what many felt, "I'm too busy with my practice to be going off marching and demonstrating." Another issue was how social problems were chosen for action when so many were being brought up at liturgy meetings of REC. By 1969, the community had grown to 125 families and when they met, the problems brought up for discussion were many and varied. Some felt that they were not doing enough on their original task, the religious education of their children. Others felt that not all ideas were being given enough discussion time, while still others felt it was the age-old question of how individuals relate to the group to which they belong. John Meis, a REC member, expressed his feelings and concluded with a prophetic statement.

We are not going to arrive anywhere as a group. Elephants, giraffes, and deer arrive in groups, but humans arrive as individuals. Love, believe, or do whatever you have to do, and then come back and share it with us at REC. We will try to accept you with your flaws. We hope you will try to accept us with our flaws. And maybe someone, within the next fifteen years, will look at us and say, "See how they love one another."

Another of the growing pains that REC members felt was apathy and opposition to its approach to social problems. When REC branched out to Winfield, where Bob Russo and Dick Nogaj lived, their meetings began to concentrate on housing discrimination that they knew existed all over DuPage County. The specific instance they found was an assemblage of substandard houses in an unincorporated area a short distance from the center of town. Bob and Dick were convinced that minorities were being excluded from the town and were living in these "shacks." REC members enlisted the mayor's help and then went to the county board, but they received no official help and even encountered resistance from county residents as word spread about what they were doing. The general attitude was that as long as the people who lived in the shacks made no noise—and none of them would for fear of eviction—it was better to leave well enough alone. This "Winfield REC" experience was one of the reasons why Dick and his wife, Florence, would later found the DuPage Branch of Habitat for Humanity.

The biggest challenge of all, however, came in June 1971 when Maryknoll College closed because of low enrollment. The REC community knew that it was just a matter of time before they would have to find a new place to meet. Because Tom Peyton was a faculty member, the College had provided free meeting space in its classrooms on Sunday mornings when regular college classes were not in session. Everyone knew that finding another meeting place for so large a group would be difficult and costly. Since REC did not have any kind of dues or collections, the only money the group had was what was collected for specific projects and needy individuals. By the end of the summer, the Maryknoll building was closed and REC had to find a new home. Thus began a period of wandering that would eventually give rise to the forerunner of the PRC.

Wandering

REC's development in the years 1971 to 1974 is not well documented. The loss of its meeting place meant that there were no longer any bulletins and, more seriously, a drop in member participation at both liturgy meetings and in social action. Tom faced his own crisis. Without his base as a faculty member at Maryknoll College, he had to find a job in order to continue working with REC. He was able to get the job of registrar at George Williams College in Downers Grove.

Finding a new meeting place proved difficult. The Glen Ellyn location of Maryknoll College was convenient because it was roughly the center of DuPage County from which most REC members came. A number of places in the immediate vicinity of the College provided short-term solutions, but none was ideal. REC met for a short time at a public school building and later at a YMCA, but these were available only on Sundays and there was rent to pay. As each move took place, fewer of the original REC members came to the liturgy meetings. With some new families joining, the membership stabilized at about fifty families. Although no bulletins were being published, a new address list was compiled and the phone network kept all informed of where home meetings would take place and what social action was being planned. No one was ever considered to have left REC, so those who no longer came to the liturgy meetings on Sundays were still contacted for social actions and events.

REC members were able to settle for a while at the Bridge, a meeting place and coffee house located on the grounds of the Franciscan Sisters Convent in Wheaton, Illinois. People who frequented the Bridge before REC were of the same ideological persuasion as REC members, but much younger. Concerns about social problems in DuPage County were topics that were already being discussed at the Bridge on a regular basis. Discussion, however, did not often lead to social action. Some REC members felt uneasy about this lack of action and the search began for something that would be more satisfying to those who sought accomplishments rather than endless talk.

Social action during this wandering period had diminished but did not cease. Support for Native Americans who were demonstrating for their rights became REC's focus. Along with the members of other groups, REC members joined in strategy sessions and provided protection for the demonstrators against anonymous threats. Still another social action during this period involved the sponsorship of two Chilean families who came to the United States as refugees from torture during the Pinochet regime. They were allowed into the United States only after REC had agreed to help them find housing and jobs and ensure their financial security. Most REC members contributed financially to the two families, but Rosie Dixon, Paul and Eileen LeFort, Bobbi Perkins, and Bob Russo maintained especially close contact with the families and helped them to obtain housing, transportation, and jobs, as well as gain citizenship. The lack of a permanent meeting place was still considered a weakness, however. It stimulated discussion and then action on finding a place that itself would be action oriented and would allow outreach to neighbors who were unaware of the needs of other residents of DuPage County. The result was the Peace and Justice Center.

2

The Roots Spread

Peace and Justice Center

THE PEACE AND JUSTICE CENTER was the second stage in the development of the People's Resource Center. It was yet another action of REC members. REC's social action initiatives were addressing the needs of the poor as well as the racial discrimination that was so prevalent in housing in DuPage County. As the number of REC members diminished after the closing of Maryknoll College in 1971, however, the pool of available volunteers for projects also diminished. Dorothy and Tom realized that they had to widen their reach into the larger community and tap the resources there if they were to have an impact in bringing about change. They first began to talk about a more formal organization at REC meetings and then, in June 1974, they opened a storefront with a sign in the window to let the world know that a Peace and Justice Center now existed in Glen Ellyn. Besides peace activities related to the lingering effects of the Vietnam War, Dorothy was especially interested in an outreach to women in DuPage County. She wanted to get information to women that would make them more conscious of their rights and better able to exercise those rights.

By November 1974, the new Center was well enough known to attract the interest of a reporter from the *Glen Ellyn News*. An article that appeared on page 3 of the newspaper on November 6 began by locating the Peace and Justice Center, "at the end of Taylor Street just beyond the underpass." Though not the middle of downtown, the location was in the incorporated village and traffic passed it daily because the underpass allowed Glen Ellynites to avoid a grade crossing at Main Street and the traffic delays commuter trains caused. Tom and Dorothy were joined initially by Rosie Dixon and Peter Neu, both of whom were members of REC, as well as by a few non–REC people.

The article quoted Dorothy, who was identified as "an interested homemaker," as saying that the Center was aimed at community education with an international perspective. The article went on to say that it had no political affiliation, no religious affiliation, no age requirement, and was completely supported by about ten people. Tom clarified further that, "We are not community organizers; we are an open forum resource group." These disclaimers were felt to be necessary because the reputation of Maryknoll College, though closed for three years, was still fresh in the minds of residents of Glen Ellyn and surrounding suburbs. Opposition to the Vietnam War, open housing, and racial equality had been espoused by students and some faculty members, especially Tom. Calling the Peace and Justice Center a "resource group" was meant to address the apprehension in Glen Ellyn that there might be some wild-eyed radical group in town.

The Center's mini library was reported to have books on peace, freedom movements, and racial struggle, with the added comment, "some of which are controversial." Its outreach included a meeting with Congressional Representative John Erlenborn and a booth at the DuPage County fair in Wheaton that had attracted more than 800 visitors. The reporter ended the article paraphrasing Tom, "There is no push, just friendly discussion and a desire to learn more through other people."

The Peace and Justice Center also asked REC members to go to events outside the DuPage area. Peace rallies and marches were happening around the country; several REC members attended one such event in Washington, D.C. In each case, the persons involved came back to report to the Center and to REC.

Support for prison reform was an important component of Dorothy McIntyre's outreach work at the Peace and Justice Center. The closing article in a magazine-sized publication on the "Pontiac

Prison Rebellion," published by the Pontiac Prisoners Support Coalition, was titled, "Let Justice Roll Down," by Dorothy. In ten double-column pages, she enumerated and quoted the various religious organizations that were demanding reform of the penal system and the end of capital punishment in the United States. The U.S. Catholic Conference, the Lutheran Church of America, the United Presbyterian Church U.S.A., the United Methodist Church, the American Friends Service Committee, and the United American Hebrew Congregations were all quoted at length. She ended the article, "The lives of the Pontiac Brothers rely on our resolve to make these words heard and come alive with our actions to support these men."

Move to Indiana Avenue

In 1975, the Peace and Justice Center moved to a small rented house on Indiana Avenue in Wheaton. REC members finally had a place to meet on Sundays and they began bringing nonperishable food because Dorothy had started giving emergency food aid to Peace and Justice Center visitors who expressed a need. They also brought used coats because some of the visitors were coming to the Center inadequately protected against the cold. The Peace and Justice Center was still providing information for its visitors, but Dorothy and her volunteers had begun to recognize another problem. Pregnant visitors did not have access to prenatal care. At first, the Center provided only counseling, but soon the need demanded more attention and basic clinical type prenatal care began to be offered. The services that were to be part of the early PRC had begun. For the next three years, these services were limited because the REC group was small and could not effectively expand its contributions to the Peace and Justice Center. All this changed in 1978.

In June 1978, Dorothy sent out a mimeographed flyer that announced a "Celebration and Decision Making Event." This initiative proved to be a turning point for the Peace and Justice Center. "After four years," Dorothy wrote, "the Center has come of age. It is connected with various regional and national peace and justice networks, presents regular informative programs on a variety of issues, collects extensive resource materials, and provides facilities for a variety of programs."

The first of the programs mentioned was the People's Resource

Center. Dorothy had actually named the PRC in the February 1978 issue of her bulletin, but at this point of "coming of age," the PRC got first billing even though she still considered it only a program for which facilities were provided. Dorothy was obviously envisioning a much larger scope for the work that had already begun as she framed decision making in a series of questions.

− Can we continue to exist with only volunteer staffing?
− Should we hire a part-time coordinator?
− Do we want to stay at the present location?
− What issues shall we deal with?
− Is there a future for a Peace and Justice Center in DuPage County?

The "present location" was the rented house in Wheaton. She also listed the annual budget of the Peace and Justice Center as $7,400. Two further questions followed:

− Can we maintain this?
− Could we expand it?

Up until this point, Dorothy had relied on REC members and her personal friends for funds. She had already decided on the answer to the last question. She would expand the operations of the Center.

No record exists of how these questions were discussed or decided, but in an undated information sheet Dorothy told newcomers that the Peace and Justice Center is currently sponsoring programs on human rights, women's issues, energy, disarmament and nuclear proliferation, senior citizen's needs, and racism. This list did not mention hunger programs, but was immediately followed by another list of "activities" that included food cooperatives and a food pantry. The transition to food distribution was going on, but slowly, and it was still an activity of the Peace and Justice Center along with warm-clothing distribution and prenatal care.

Again, there is no record of this development, but at some point in late 1978 or early 1979, Dorothy announced that nonperishable food would be given out at the Peace and Justice Center. Later she reported in a bulletin that the first week of distribution attracted only five visitors. Within a short time, probably a few months, the number of visitors had jumped to over a hundred families who were coming on a once-a-month basis. This volume demanded much more organization and a great deal more in contributions of both grocery staples and money. Within a year of her first mention of the PRC, Dorothy was writing both a newsletter and a bulletin that were devoted exclusively to the People's Resource Center. The Peace and Justice Center quietly reinvented itself to concentrate on needs that had been all but invisible and silent up to that time in DuPage County. Peace activities, however, had never completely ended for REC members. While the military draft continued REC members did draft counseling and participated in antiwar rallies. Fast forward almost forty years to the second decade of the twenty-first century, and Frank and Kay Goetz, still members of REC, are part of the West Suburban Faith-Based Peace Coalition and the Peace Alliance. Peace and other social issues are discussed monthly at the Coffee House that Frank has organized in the offices of another REC couple, Dick and Florence Nogaj.

In this transition period, 1978–1979, as the Peace and Justice Center morphed into the People's Resource Center, an emphasis on women's issues remained strong. Since some REC members such as Ruth Riha and Fran Holtzman were already active in women's organizations, outreach to women was a natural course of social action. The struggle to get the Equal Rights Amendment ratified focused on peace and justice activities. As more women came to the Peace and Justice Center, it became obvious that health issues were high on the list of their needs. Providing food, clothing, and basic medical needs became the focus that rapidly consumed the time and energies of Dorothy and her growing cadre of volunteers.

The evolution of the People's Resource Center followed the pattern of its grandparent, REC. Identifying and acting on one problem inevitably led to the discovery of another. Though poverty was a main issue for REC members' social actions, hunger did not become a pressing issue until women began coming to the Peace and Justice Center for prenatal physical examinations. Once the need for better nutrition became obvious, another social action began. Hunger may truly be said to be *the* reason why the People's Resource Center was founded, and food distribution continues to be a prime social action of the Center.

Late in 1979 and into 1980, three centers—Religious Education Center (REC), Peace and Justice Center (P/J Center), and People's Resource Center (PRC)—were all functioning under one roof. REC, with its Sunday liturgy meetings, was the support group Dorothy knew she could always rely upon. P/J Center was attracting clients and the PRC was providing for their physical and medical needs.

Clients waiting for food distribution
outside the house on Indiana Avenue, late 1970s

3

Years of Formation, 1975–1992

People's Resource Center Founded

WHEN DOROTHY MCINTYRE first used the name "People's Resource Center" in her newsletter of February 1978, she stated the goal of the new center and showed the relationship to its parent organization.

> The People's Resource Center of the Peace and Justice Center is a coalition of people working together to establish a resource center in the west suburban area. Our goal is to provide an alternative structure for learning, working, teaching, sharing and encouraging change. Our prime focus is on services to women. We will work alone or in cooperation with other persons and organizations to do any of the activities necessary to fulfill our goal.

She did not explain why this new organization should be a separate entity within the Peace and Justice Center but her focus on "services for women" seemed to indicate that the Peace and Justice Center could not adequately address the needs of the women who had come to it. She introduced her coordinating committee, all women. Besides herself, Dorothy named Charlotte Littlewood, a member of REC, and Barbara Nichols, Mary Tworek-Tupper, and Jeanne Crilly. Later, when Jeanne and Mary left the committee, they were replaced by Rosali Placet and Jan Tyler, both REC members.

Dorothy's first newsletters stressed the formative stage of the new Center and asked for "ideas, suggestions, and feelings about what we are doing." The newsletter was to inform people about services, activities, and events that were locally available from governmental agencies, social service organizations, churches, and educational institutions. Although there is no membership list for this initial stage of the PRC's development, Dorothy referred to "our members" and described their various backgrounds, "business persons, homemakers, students, professionals, religious, and blue collar workers." The primary objective of the first meetings was to establish a need for coordination and dissemination of information about what services were available to women in DuPage County. Finally, in order to make sure that no one worried about the cost of using the PRC, Dorothy stressed, "Our efforts are completely volunteer and funded only by donations. There is no charge for services or programs at PRC."

In October 1978, the newsletter announced additional services.

So—beginning October 12, and every Thursday thereafter (except Thanksgiving) between 4:30 and 9:30 p.m. we will be staffed by professionals (psychiatric nurse or psychiatric social worker or counselor) and trained volunteers.... Our professional staff is capable of working with such problems as domestic violence, personal or family problems, persons experiencing depressive feelings, persons coping with aging parents, or other related problems.

A second new service was to provide a place of "peace, quiet, and the availability of a bottomless coffee/tea pot." Once again, a need had made itself known while the staff was collecting and trying to disseminate information. Dorothy's determination to get every possible bit of information published is illustrated in a note in one of the newsletters/calendars. "The last page of the calendar is empty. This bothers me. Would you send material to fill this page."

It is interesting to note that in the first issues of this PRC newsletter, there was no mention of food distribution even though regular distribution of food began sometime in the middle of 1978. It was not until March of 1979 that a complete list of PRC services

was given and food was mentioned: The PRC is a completely volunteer service—provided for women by women. The PRC:
- Publishes a monthly calendar of events.
- Operates a telephone referral service to place women in contact with existing community resources. (This is *not* a crisis line.) Call Monday through Friday from 10 a.m. to 3 p.m.
- Staffs a weekly open-house evening on Thursdays from 4:30 p.m. to 9:30 p.m., where women can come to talk read, think, or get away.
- We provide a potluck supper for women who come by during the supper hour.
- Operates an emergency food pantry that can supply canned goods and nonperishable foodstuffs for immediate short-term help.

The first handouts of food by the Peace and Justice Center in 1975 had been on an informal basis to take care of particular individuals' needs. Three years later the PRC began operation and food distribution became a formal service of the organization.

Production of the newsletter's four mimeographed pages each month was a strain on the women involved and on the finances of the organization. Bobbie Perkins, a REC member, came to Dorothy's aid by offering to print the legal-sized sheets where she worked. Dorothy wrote of her, "Bobbie who can print and have root canal work done on the same day and still leave hilarious notes for us."

Initial distribution of the newsletter/calendar was to libraries, bookstores, and organizations that were strongly women oriented and already had ties to the Peace and Justice Center. Later, distribution included the College of DuPage (COD), the Public Aid Office in Wheaton, and even apartment houses. The members of the coordinating committee were convinced that the services listed in the newsletter needed to be more widely known to be of value to those who came to the Center. As months passed, the PRC advertised its own programs, but making services known continued to be a problem that needed mentioning. Dorothy wrote:

But even with the mailings and the work that many women are doing, there are still about 100 calendars left at the end of the month. They are doing us no good sitting around the Center. Stop by and pick up a few extra ones and take them with you. We have had very good feedback on them so be happy to spread the joy around.

By 1981, she reported that 9,000 newsletter/calendars had been distributed, and about half of the people who came to the Center had learned about the services from these publications.

Funding costs for distribution were a constant source of concern. Center volunteers such as Eileen LeFort and Barbara Nichols delivered bulk packages of the newsletter in their own cars, but mailing required postage. The Center first asked for a $2-per-year donation to defray the mailing costs. This was later raised to $5 per year. No one who wanted to receive the newsletter, was dropped from the mailing list, however. Dorothy's attitude was that the calendar was a service and access to it would not depend on ability to pay.

Women's Health

The variety of services offered by the People's Resource Center drew women to the house on Indiana Avenue. Their needs became apparent as they talked to the staff. Psychological counseling proved to be necessary, but was only one part of the larger health problems many of the women faced. As the demand for prenatal services increased, malnutrition was recognized as a problem for expectant mothers.

Dorothy and her volunteer committee discussed the prenatal care problem and at first shied away from becoming directly involved in medical care. As they talked with visitors to the Center, however, they found more and more women who were getting no prenatal care. Those women would simply wait for labor pains and then go to an emergency room and face whatever difficulties they and their newborns had. For the next few years, the major services of the PRC were prenatal care and food distribution in that order.

The prenatal care program was serving women in serious financial need. Dorothy had to recruit doctors and nurses as volunteers because the PRC was operating on a shoestring. She also brought in students from Illinois Benedictine College as interns to provide support for the medical professionals. A rear bedroom of the house was transformed into a very simple "clinic." As word of this clinic spread, obstetricians at Central DuPage Hospital reacted. Their concern led them to ask Dorothy to explain, at a meeting with her and Paul LeFort, what was going on at the PRC. Dorothy began the meeting by asking the doctors what she could do to address their concerns. She ended by signing some of them up to volunteer at the clinic. That rear bedroom became the first home of the DuPage Community Clinic that would be part of the PRC until it became an entity in its own right in 1990.

In 1984, the decision was taken to hire a nurse practitioner from the Illinois Benedictine College nursing program to provide basic prenatal screening and health care in the house in Wheaton. She was also asked to plan a Health Care Delivery Service. The Health Promotion Service, as it was later renamed, became a program of the PRC. A brochure described the services available: screening physical examinations, blood/urine screening, pap smear pelvic examinations, limited prenatal care, appraisal of health hazards, and health education. Beyond these services performed at the PRC, referrals were made to the DuPage Physicians Medical Assistance Program and other appropriate care providers. Later, after it had overcome its reservations about this upstart facility, the DuPage County Health Department began to accept clients who were referred from the PRC's Health Promotion Service. Because the nurse practitioner was being paid and lab tests had to be paid for, the Health Promotion Service had to begin charging fees, but these were on a sliding scale based on a woman's ability to pay. Students from Illinois Benedictine College interviewed the women patients, put together a video, and led sessions in which problems were discussed with the clients and solutions were offered.

Carol McHaley, who had begun volunteering at the PRC in 1983, became involved in the health care activities. Since Dorothy and her committee did not want to wait for women to drop in for help, they decided to seek out women they had heard were in need and transport them to the clinic. Carol was asked to drive to West Chicago and find women who had either called in or had been mentioned by those clients who were able to get to the Center on their own. Because many of the poorer women in West Chicago were Hispanic, there was hesitancy to respond when Carol showed up at their door. However, when she announced that she was from the PRC and was there to take a woman to the Center for prenatal care, she often transported not only the woman but also a couple of children. As word spread that the PRC was a comfortable, safe, and welcoming place, the numbers of clients grew.

The growing numbers who came for health care and food—and the fact that they were lining up outside a rather rundown house —began to raise eyebrows in Wheaton. Carol remembered that often as clients were coming in, Wheaton police officers in cars were watching from the gas station next door. It took a while before the Wheaton police were satisfied that nothing suspicious was going on. At about this time Dorothy was asked about the initials "PRC" since they were the same as those being used by the People's Republic of China. Was she afraid that some might misunderstand the Center's activities? Her answer seemed to indicate that she had thought about the issue. She said, simply, "If that's the way they take it, so be it."

The work of the Health Promotion Service went on and expanded. Equipment, including a real examination table and a

(l-r) Carol McHaley, director of the DuPage
Community Clinic and Dorothy McIntyre, mid 1980s

reliable scale, were bought and the back bedroom of the rented house took on a more clinical appearance. The PRC has records of paying salaries to at least two nurse practitioners along with paying bills for lab tests. Finally, in the late 1980s, the DuPage County Health Department set up a prenatal clinic for residents in need. Carol McHaley was convinced that the example set by the PRC was an important stimulus for this innovation.

The Health Promotion Service did not die. Rather, it evolved into the DuPage Community Clinic (DCC) in May 1989. This new clinic continued to use the back bedroom of the house, but it was available to all, not just women, in need of health care. It opened only on Saturdays because that was the only day Dr. Charles Ahn was available. He and his two sons provided the first volunteer medical staff physicians for the DCC. Carol became the director of the Clinic, and later, when the DCC was formally spun off as a separate organization she became its first executive director.

The DuPage Community Clinic was not the only group to develop out of the PRC. As previously mentioned, another problem that demanded attention arose while the PRC was providing care for women, abuse. An abused woman in DuPage County had no safe place to go when she finally decided to flee an abusing spouse. A friend of Ruth Riha, a REC member, appeared at her door one morning and told Ruth that she needed a place where her husband could not find her. Ruth was able to give her temporary shelter, but enlisted another REC member, Eleanor Tlusty, to search for a more permanent solution to the problem. They visited shelters in neighboring Kane and Will counties and were amazed to find that those shelters were fully equipped and staffed. DuPage County had no such shelter. At the YWCA Ruth and Eleanor searched for other women willing to help and together they founded the Family Shelter Service of DuPage County, with Eleanor as its first board president. Beginning as a safe environment for women who had nowhere else to turn, the shelter went on to offer job training, relationship negotiations, and some legal and educational services. It continues in existence today.

The reference to a "psychiatric nurse or social worker" in one of Dorothy's earlier newsletters was not explained. However, the presence of such professionals was clearly a response to yet another problem. As abused women came to the center and told their stories, the word "rape" began to come up. A REC member, Carol Roller, had started a group called DuPage Women Against Rape (DWAR) in 1971. She began with education courses for hospital workers and police officers and developed both a Rape Hotline and a Rape Survivors support group. Carol worked with Dorothy and the committee to put rape victims who came to the Center in touch with the resources they needed. The psychiatric nurse and social worker were their first point of contact. Though the DWAR never became an official program of the People's Resource Center, Carol's expertise and contacts were a significant contribution to the women's health initiative of the Center.

Serving women was a prime focus of the early PRC. Programs included education about nutrition and money matters and a book club. A Gray Panthers affiliate also organized there and used the center for its meetings. Since the PRC was started by women and run primarily by them, just about everything that went on there had something to do with women's inequality of status, power, and possessions. The October 1979 issue of the *Bulletin,* which Dorothy and the coordinating committee distributed, contained a number of quotes relating to women. One stood out because it was timely and because it was written by a famous man:

> Menial employed servants were available only to a minority of the pre-industrial population; the servant-wife is available, democratically, to almost the entire present male population.
> — John Kenneth Galbraith, *The Economics of the American Housewife* (1973)

Early Board of Directors

Before the People's Resource Center was legally incorporated in Illinois in October 1980, Dorothy had an informal board consisting of the volunteers who worked with her. Mary Ann Bostwick was president of this board. After incorporation, the first minutes from a board of directors meeting were dated October 11, 1981. The directors were all REC members, Paul LeFort, Rosalie Placet, Constance Gardner, and Gene Ring, who acted as pro tem chair and secretary. It is interesting to note that in conversation, Dorothy described the ideal image of the board as being client based. Yet, when the selection had to be made, she chose people she knew, REC members.

This first board meeting took care of legal requirements for the newly registered organization. Bylaws were adopted, the articles of incorporation were approved, and the Bank of Wheaton was designated as repository for corporate funds. Other REC members given authorization to sign checks were Charlotte Sommer and Margaret Roth. The new corporation's address was listed as 107 West Indiana, Wheaton, and the property was designated a rental property for which $420.00 per month was being paid.

The next board of directors meeting for which minutes exist was on October 24, 1982. Since the PRC now had a tax-exemption number and was eligible to receive federal government commodities, it had gained legal recognition as a not-for-profit. The first line of these 1982 minutes mentioned the Campaign for Human Development (CHD), a Roman Catholic program to provide aid to those in need. The next item was a report by the treasurer that $4,100 still remained from the CHD grant. This was then a substantial portion of the total PRC budget.

Another item in the minutes pertained to one of the volunteers, Janice Cagel, who was also a member of the board. The decision mentioned represented a major change in direction from the way Dorothy had run the PRC before the board of directors was formed.

> Use of salary as budgeted in the C.H.D. grant was discussed. Director of the program is refusing a salary at present and wants the money circulated to pay the expenses of the people who use the pantry and volunteer at the People's Resource Center. These volunteers assist with the running of the Center programs presented in the grant. The board decided to pay for expenses incurred by the volunteers and for reimbursement for time spent in working with the C.H.D. programs. Those who are on public aid must work within state and federal guidelines.

The director mentioned was Dorothy. She had been working for eight years with the Peace and Justice Center and the PRC without any compensation. She felt strongly that all work should be volunteer and she was initially opposed to hiring any paid staff. She felt, however, that Janice Cagel's situation was an exception. Not all volunteers were financially able to work without compensation.

Janice had become a volunteer after having been a client. Dorothy's letter, published in the section on food, details a situation that would be repeated often at the PRC.

The minutes of this board meeting made it clear that the growth of the PRC was necessitating more expenditures. The subject of producing a brochure was discussed and then tabled. Two more discussions also involved spending money.

Additional items on the board agenda included (1) the need for more volunteers and staffing; (2) the need for additional staff "as the Center expands its service to the community"; and (3) the need for more office help.

The other money item discussed was liability insurance. The new board did not trust the landlord's insurance to cover the heavy usage of the rented house. Between health care and food distribution, there were plenty of possibilities for insurance claims by both clients and volunteers.

One interesting item in these minutes was the "need for a tenant to live at the People's Resource Center." No background is given, but the fact that Tom Peyton had left the United States for an assignment in Hong Kong the previous year would seem to be the occasion for this discussion. He had lived in an attic room after the Peace and Justice Center moved from Glen Ellyn to Wheaton. His salary as registrar at George Williams College had provided some income for the PRC from the rent he paid. Up until his departure, he had continued to minister to REC when it met at the house on Sunday mornings. Although he was not mentioned in any of the documents that Dorothy issued, Tom's ministry had had a strong influence on REC and consequently on the direction of the PRC.

The next board meeting for which minutes exist is dated December 11, 1983. In this meeting, the board took up two main concerns, health programs and Christmas Gift distribution. Two guests made a presentation suggesting that the Center expand its health care activities to include a counseling program for disabled persons. Since the house could be entered only by climbing stairs either front or rear, the board stated that access would have to be limited to ambulatory clients. The other health concern was the "health needs survey" that REC member Phil Chinn had compiled. As a result of this survey, Paul LeFort was assigned to teach two of the volunteers how to do data entry using his computer.

Christmas of 1983 loomed large for the board at this December meeting. Janice Cagel reported on the December 4 Christmas party at Southminster Presbyterian Church for families who were using the pantry. Eighty-five people attended. Janice also reported on the Thanksgiving dinner for thirty-five to forty pantry users. The dinner was a potluck buffet for which the Center staff prepared two turkeys with all the fixings. Another item presaged the PRC Christmas programs that would evolve later.

The People's Resource Center will prepare to supply seventy-five families with Christmas baskets. Janice Cagel will prepare a food list. Gyrtha Smith's sons will volunteer to help with the project. The Youth Group from Southminster Church will also volunteer time to decorate and pack food baskets.

It is not known whether Gyrtha Smith's sons or the youth group knew they were going to volunteer, but it was obvious that Janice Cagel was very much involved in the holiday activities of the PRC.

Still another indicator of things to come was a short entry in the meeting's minutes relating to clients. "We will start a new filing system for intake for the pantry." The names of clients seeking food had been recorded, but by 1983, their numbers had increased to the point that a more formal record keeping system was needed. The number of clients was used to let potential donors know what the PRC was doing.

As was to be expected, board minutes from 1982 on included a number of items relating to funding. Evolving as it had from the Peace and Justice Center, the PRC had operated on individual contributions until after its incorporation in 1980. Most of this early support came from REC members and their friends. Some individual support came from people who had heard about the Center and wanted to help. An example is a letter from July 1982 signed simply "Nancy."

I have been quite distressed the past two years by the growing disinterest on the part of the Government in the health of its own citizens. This past paycheck, I saw my tax cut for the first time. I am most anxious that this unwelcome windfall not be spent on material things but rather on providing the necessities to people who are suffering most under this insane policy. Therefore, I plan to continue to send a similar amount to you from each paycheck I get in the foreseeable future.

Despite individual donations like Nancy's, Dorothy and the board understood well that larger amounts of money were going to be needed to continue the PRC's work. Grant writing began in February of 1982.

The first application was for the grant, previously mentioned, from the Campaign for Human Development of the Catholic Diocese of Joliet. The application was for $16,550 over two years. The PRC's budget for the first year alone was given as $22,690. The services to be funded were financial counseling, nutrition education, income tax assistance, single parent support groups, and health education and evaluation. The basic reason given for the needs in these areas was unemployment triggered by cutbacks in federal assistance programs.

The grant was received and an interim report was sent to the Diocese of Joliet. However, the grant had to be supplemented by the first ventures of the PRC into fund-raising events. These included a Brown Bag Yard Sale, which netted $425, and a performance by Marion Wade, called "An Evening of Song," which raised $200. Southminster Presbyterian Church also sent the proceeds of a special collection to the PRC.

In 1983, the Federal Emergency Manpower Act (FEMA) gave the PRC a grant for $7,000 to cover emergency housing assistance. This was reported to have provided 2,000 days of shelter for families. As part of the background for housing assistance, Barbara Nichols had assembled photographs of the "abominable conditions that some families are living in."

By February 1984, another grant proposal had been written to the Campaign for Human Development asking for $10,000 for expanded health promotional services. Part of this money was needed for equipment, such as an examination table, for the growing Health Care Program. The focus of the PRC from 1982 to 1984 had been primarily on health concerns. Though food distribution was going on, it had not been the primary request in grant proposals. A note at the end of the board's February 1984 minutes seems to indicate the beginning of rapid expansion of the food distribution program.

The work at the Center has increased. We are in need of additional help for the office and pantry. In January, the Pantry was able to serve 190 families: 352 adults and 389 children. The total number of persons served was 741.

This two-pronged attack on health and food needs was taxing both the funds and the personnel of the PRC. The food distribution program would slowly become the dominant activity of the Center.

Food

The emergencies that occasioned the first food distribution after the Peace and Justice Center moved to the house in Wheaton were job losses, home fires, or unexpected family break ups. This REC social action effort was not organized beyond storing the food in the basement of the house and answering a need when it became known.

As the People's Resource Center attracted women to its programs, especially its prenatal screening, malnutrition of women, and sometimes of their children, became a need that had to be addressed. The subsequent increase in demand for food meant that the informality of the initial distribution gave way to an organized effort that entailed regular purchases of food from Aldi, the Bethlehem Center, and the Northern Illinois Food Bank. Purchase of food, in turn, led to the need for a tax-exemption status. After 1982, having secured tax-exemption status, Dorothy enlisted Fran Holtzman and Margaret Roth to act as buyers. She asked Margaret to be the "treasurer," a job that had only two functions: (1) writing checks for food delivered and to cover medical tests for clients, and (2) reminding REC members that the PRC needed more money.

By late 1982, the number of people coming to the Center was taxing the coordinating committee as they tried to cope with regular rounds of medical care, activities for women, and distribution of food. In December, two men showed up in search of food. They did not want a handout, they were willing to work for what they received. Dorothy put both to work in the basement as stock clerks to receive deliveries and to conduct distribution that was then taking place on a weekly basis. One of the two, Al White, stayed with the PRC and, at thirty years, is the longest serving volunteer-then-employee of the Center. Al remembered that in his first year of distributing boxes of food through the basement window he was serving fifty to sixty clients a week. He soon became a familiar sight to those who came for food. His experience of being in need himself made for an easy rapport with those who came to the window, even though most saw only his head and shoulders as he handed up a box of groceries.

The story of client turned volunteer-then-employee has not been uncommon at the PRC. In January 1984, however, Janice Cagel became the first person to receive a paycheck as an employee. In an undated letter, Janice wrote:

> I am a single parent and have one child. I came to People's Resource Center last Spring when the Center was involved in the cheese distribution program. I am unemployed though I look for work every week. I have no one to care for my child so any job that I find has to pay me enough to pay for child care. I am on public assistance and receive food stamps. I can just make it. If I had more children I don't think that I could manage. It helps me to know that the Center is here in case I have a real emergency. I volunteer at the center. I feel that I increase my own self-respect when I help others. I helped or-

Food delivery through the living room window
on Indiana Avenue, late 1970s

ganize the Brown Bag Yard Sale this summer. The sale helped provide good school clothing for many needy families. I worked out in the community contacting families to get them to participate in the sale. I like doing community work. I have met many people. Just working this fall with the recent federal cheese distribution program I worked with over forty families. I helped plan and work with the nutrition program. I know how hard it is to make it and have learned to be a very careful shopper and food manager. I want to have the chance to share some of my skills with other mothers. I am concerned about the health of these women and their children and want to help them to begin to learn to be independent. I volunteer at the Center because it is one place where I can work and know that my child is welcome. This is very important to me.

Dorothy probably asked for this letter for one of two reasons, to recruit other volunteers or to show the board that this woman should be on the payroll.

The cheese distribution program Janice mentions was an indication that the PRC's pantry had already been recognized by an agency of the federal government. Cheese was a commodity that the U.S. Department of Agriculture had bought up to stabilize prices for dairy farmers. In the early 1980s, the stored cheese was distributed and certified charitable organizations were eligible to receive it. The cheese came in large blocks and was delivered by truck every few weeks. Storage was at first a problem because the amount of cheese delivered filled most of the basement space dedicated to nonperishables. A wrapped block of cheese was routinely included in the box of food clients received. Later, other commodities were delivered with the cheese and the arrival of the truck meant that volunteers had to mobilize quickly to unload it. This program continued into the 1990s.

By 1984, the food distribution program had become a smooth-running operation, such that it was given very little space in board minutes for April of that year. One item refers to Janice Cagel: "Janice suggested we put a phone in the basement. Dorothy said she could grant-write if Janice and Darlene ran the pantry." There was no further explanation, but the implication was that Dorothy

(left) Al White at the basement window for food
distribution

(below) Client picking up
food from the basement
window

wanted to dedicate more time to fund-raising and felt that the pantry
operation was big enough now to demand two managers. What is
most significant about the board Minutes from this period is the lack
of reference to food distribution. Almost all the discussion by board
members centers around health issues and programs, despite the fact
that the food census for December 1983 listed 212 families served, a
total of 887 individuals. These numbers suggest that volunteers
were needed at least three days a week for buying food, packaging
it in boxes, and distributing the boxes on Tuesday mornings.

The April board minutes provide yet another glimpse of the
food program. Katy Bruce of the Southminster Presbyterian
Church of Glen Ellyn planned an Easter party for the "pantry people." The party was expected to be large enough to require the
space the church could provide rather than the very limited space
of the house on Indiana Avenue. This item in the minutes is followed by the statement, "Joe McHaley agreed to be on the board."
Joe McHaley, Carol's husband, was an assistant pastor at Southminster and his board position strengthened the ties that already
existed between the PRC and the church.

Clothing

One of the oldest services of the People's Resource Center was
called simply, the "Clothes Closet." It began quietly almost as

soon as the PRC came into existence. As with other services, it arose out of the obvious needs of women who came to the Center for medical care and food. In winter, the lack of adequate coats clients were wearing was remarked by volunteers, especially when the clients had to stand in line outside the house for a while. The story was that an unnamed woman donor brought a bag of clothes after seeing the clients in line. Two volunteers, Audrey Burke and Fran Holtzman, the codirectors of the project, sorted and distributed the clothing. Fran then started to ask fellow REC members and other friends for the usable clothing they no longer needed. Response was immediate and almost overwhelming.

The first problem was, as always, storage space. The clothing had to be sorted by size, gender, and age. To be useful, it also had to fit the season. Fran and Audrey soon found that donors cleaned out their home closets as the seasons changed. Summer clothes came in abundantly at the end of summer and winter clothes showed up in April. The only place in the house to keep clothes was in the basement where they competed for space with the food that was waiting to be distributed. By the early 1980s, all the pipes in the basement were hung with donated clothing. Because the clients came into the basement to choose clothing, the appropriate sea-

Clothes Closet volunteer directors, (l-r) Fran Holtzman
and Audrey Burke, Roosevelt Road, mid 1990s

sonal clothes had to be easily available. As the selection became greater, clients spent more time trying to decide what they wanted to take. At first, Fran and Audrey told people to take whatever they wanted, but this approach meant that all the best items were taken early in a week and those clients who came later had little or nothing to choose from.

Fran and Audrey then devised a point system based on the size of the client's family. Infants' and children's clothes were always in demand as were men's shirts and pants. Trying to insure equitable distribution proved to be a full-time and often stressful job for the two women. They were joined by other volunteers, including REC members Kay Goetz, Eileen LeFort, and Ruth Riha. As time went on, the "system" worked fairly smoothly. Excess items or those that were not in good enough condition to be given out were bagged and held for pickup by the St. Vincent de Paul Society or Goodwill Industries. Later, donations included small toys and household items. These items made storage space problems even worse, but since they did not fall under the point system they disappeared rather quickly.

Because the selection of clothes put the volunteers in closer

Volunteer Ruth Fitzgerald in the Clothes Closet

contact with clients than did food distribution, stories emerged from the volunteers' experiences. On a cold November day, Ruth Riha, working in the Clothes Closet, had given one young woman baby clothes and asked the mother where she had put her coat. The woman said that she only needed baby clothes and she did not have a coat. Ruth was shocked and remembered a good coat that had just come in. She got it for the woman and then had to convince her that it was hers to take. The woman left wearing her new coat and wiping tears from her eyes.

One of the many stories Fran Holtzman told was about another young woman who picked out a wedding dress that had just been donated. Fran asked her when was the wedding going to be and the woman responded, "I don't know, but I hope to be married some day."

It was the experiences of volunteers in the Clothes Closet that led the PRC to expand its Christmas giving program, which had started as a Christmas party. The program was to grow into "Share the Spirit" and eventually required the use of a large building on the DuPage County fairgrounds, where hundreds of clients received children's toys, hats, scarves, mittens, and books.

Donations and Funding

The end of the 1980s was a time of continued growth in the programs of the PRC. Unfortunately, documentation for this period is almost nonexistent, in part because of two floods that destroyed documents stored in the basement. The need for additional help demanded more paid staff and food distribution had gone way beyond the in-kind donations of REC members and other friends of the PRC. Dorothy was spending more time managing the growing operations in each program and looking for institutional and foundation money. She contacted churches in DuPage County, especially in Wheaton and Glen Ellyn, and she started an informal speakers' group to deliver the message of the People's Resource Center to congregations on Sunday mornings. Many pastors proved open to having a speaker and taking a collection for the work despite the fact that the PRC had no church affiliation. Dorothy also contacted Boy Scout and Girl Scout troops and schools at all levels. Banks became corporate donors and the U.S. Post Office launched a food collection effort that filled the pantry during the

PRC's May drive. One sidelight of the Post Office collection was the comment of one postal worker after he had brought food into the basement. Every square inch was packed floor to ceiling and he stood back and said, "This should last quite a while." He was a bit taken back when the pantry volunteer replied, "Yes, about two weeks."

Schools, especially St. Francis High School in Wheaton, were strong supporters of the Christmas program. Soliciting gifts for the Christmas program in the late 1980s, Dorothy gave the number of children in each family as well as their genders and ages and schools took this information and ran inter-classroom contests to see who could come up with the most presents. Students wrapped their gifts in Christmas paper and delivered them to the Center. St. Francis had to rent a fairly large truck to deliver the gifts. The house on Indiana Avenue seemed a lot smaller as every room filled with the brightly wrapped packages. At the same time, the REC group was using its Sunday meetings to wrap gifts that REC members themselves had contributed and those that had come in from other individuals and stores. A Kmart truck pulled up one day and unloaded a large load of toy trucks that looked exactly like the delivery truck. Every child in every family had at least a truck to play with for Christmas.

The overwhelming response to the Christmas appeal each year finally led to the need to control the flow of gifts because there was not enough space to store them and because of the vast differences between the number of gifts designated for each family. The first problem was solved by temporarily renting space at the DuPage County fairgrounds to store and then give out the gifts. The problem of inequality was expressed graphically in an observation by a volunteer: "I saw one family fill the trunk of a car with gifts that had been brought in by high school students, while another family left with only two used sweaters."

This problem was later solved when Lyn Conway set up "Share the Spirit" and the requests went out for unwrapped gifts that were then distributed on the basis of family size as each family came to the fairgrounds. REC members and high school students who had really enjoyed wrapping gifts were not too pleased with the new distribution method, but all agreed that it was the only fair way to handle the generosity of people around Christmas.

Beside money and Christmas gifts, the PRC developed a base of in-kind and labor donors whose contributions were difficult to catalog but who were nonetheless very important. Companies like Sara Lee and Lucent sent groups of volunteers to the Center for work in the Food Pantry and later in the Computer Literacy programs. Women's clubs and guilds, residents of retirement homes, members of service organizations and credit unions all provided goods and services that ranged from knitted stocking caps and bicycles to bags of personal care products that were given to clients when they received food. Baby needs, strollers, and car seats came in and were often given out before they could be put on a shelf.

Pretzels and candy were donated for the children who accompanied their parents to the Food Pantry and bakeries donated bread that had not been sold by late afternoon. Farmers from the surrounding area brought in fresh produce in season and these vegetables and fruits were added to the bags of nonperishables clients carried out of the Center.

Labor was provided for the Center by groups such as the Elmhurst Garden Club, whose members arrived on a Saturday morning and cleaned up the landscape around the house and planted flowers. As space limitations became more and more of a problem, volunteers came in and built shelves to ease some of the crowding in the pantry. One important suggestion came from Kay McKeen of the DuPage Recycling Center. She suggested that the PRC look into the discards that came from big box stores in the county. She told Warren Roth and he began visiting local Target Stores and talking to managers. Within a short time, he was filling his car every Tuesday with paper products, personal care products, and diapers that would have otherwise been thrown out by these stores because of mislabeling or slightly damaged packaging. The diapers were especially in demand because they were expensive and not a regular item distributed through the pantry. These pickups were later extended to other stores, including Walmart and many food stores. This effort continues to the present in both Wheaton and Westmont.

In 1990, a volunteer at the Center recorded verbal or written comments that accompanied donations of money, goods, and labor to the Center. This abbreviated list is a group portrait of a good part of the PRC's donor base.

- "My spouse and I no longer cook or eat at home."
- "I had to get rid of food because I developed an allergy."
- "I cleaned out the house of my parents after they moved into a retirement home."
- "I read about the pantry in the paper, I had no idea that there was so much poverty in DuPage."
- "I shopped at Aldi's and Sam's Club all morning to help you out."
- Employees of the Department of Probation and Court Services could dress casually on Fridays as long as they brought in food for the Center during the week.
- "The kids have grown out of diapers and baby clothes."
- "I always give when I visit my parents in Wheaton."
- Employees at different local companies organized food and clothing drives and asked companies to match their contributions.
- Snacks and desserts came in from organizations that had an oversupply after their seminars or workshops.
- Mugs and cups were given for the same reason.
- United Airlines gave an oversupply of blankets.

The *Wheaton Leader* published a story about the PRC on March 17, 1993, under the byline of Norlyn Egbert. One part of the article deserves retelling here because it showed that the PRC was not just another agency. Its spirit touched even young hearts.

Two first grade girls at Sandberg School in Wheaton wanted to help the poor. They made rosewater perfume and sold it to their neighbors in waxed paper cups for 5 cents each. They raised $1.20, which they sent with a note to the Center. Dorothy was touched by the heartfelt gesture and invited them to an Open House for Sponsors only. Not only did they show up with their parents, but one set of grandparents joined them from Arlington Heights.

The two girls were Megan Machenbrock and Emily Schlickman. Emily's mother, Sandee, was a volunteer at the Center and her father, Andy, was asked to join the PRC board of directors. He became the first attorney on the board. Emily, as a teenager, returned to the PRC as a volunteer.

By 1992, the PRC's formation period was drawing to a close. The food pantry was a well-known and well-used service that had become, for many, synonymous with the PRC. The DuPage Community Clinic had grown into an entity of its own, though it was still sharing space with the PRC, and the Clothes Closet, in its cramped basement quarters, was open to all who came for food. The "Turkey Giveaway" program, which had started small, had become a source for clients to rely upon at both Thanksgiving and Christmas. The Christmas gift program that Lyn and Pete Conway had started out of St. Michael's Church in Wheaton had split into "Share the Spirit for Christmas" and "Adopt a Family," a year-round program for families who had encountered a particular hardship, such as chronic illness, and needed extra income for a period of time. Dorothy summed up this growth in a September 1992 letter to sponsors:

> In 1990 about 400 of our food pantry patrons requested help through the "Share the Spirit" giving program; in 1991 this number jumped up to 600 families. The "Adopt a Family' program that provides a special monthly food supplement to

Old house on Indiana Avenue. Painting by Bob Dwyer

families has increased from one family in 1989 to 20 families in 1991. It is truly amazing that all of this is being accomplished by two part-time paid staff and 16-18 volunteers a week.

She added, "On days the food pantry is distributing boxes of groceries, the lines begin to form hours before we are open." She concluded with a revelation that would launch the next phase of the PRC's growth. "We dreamed of a home with more space…We have found a spacious new home!!!" Dorothy could not dream, much less foretell, the tumultuous series of changes that the next four years would bring.

4

Years of Change, 1992–1995

Joy And Sorrow

DOROTHY MCINTYRE'S ORIGINAL IDEA—that the PRC should be a "center" where those who had resources could share with those who needed them—became a reality as the PRC matured in the late 1980s and early 1990s. With maturity came challenges, however. One of the challenges was a rent increase. The owner of the rented house had expressed mixed feelings about its use. At one point in the late 1980s, he had asked for a significant increase in the rent. At that time, the PRC was just able to make rent payments and other expenses with the donations and grants that were then coming in. After negotiations with the landlord forestalled the increase, Dorothy knew that she had to find a place where rent would not be a constant worry. She, and Carol, began a search that was to take a couple of years but brought them to a much bigger building on Roosevelt Road.

New Home

In early 1990, Dorothy had made a firm decision to leave the house on Indiana Avenue. She was looking for a place that was not only larger but also had features the PRC and the DuPage Community Clinic (DCC) needed. These features included a large waiting room, private office space, rooms that could be converted into medical examining rooms, and a basement for food storage and distribution. Outside, the building also had to have adequate parking. There was even a larger need that Dorothy was all too aware of. She did not have anywhere near the amount of money necessary to purchase her "dream" building and she had no prospect of getting that kind of money soon. In line with the PRC tradition, Dorothy was to rely on not one but two miracles. As usual, they came to pass.

The PRC was then pretty well known in DuPage County and there were people in County government who were sympathetic to the Center's needs in serving the county's growing number of poor residents. Dorothy found out about Community Development Block Grants (CDBG), which the federal government would give to a local government for its area of jurisdiction. She found that CDBG money could be used to purchase a building, but ownership remained in the hands of the local government. A long-term lease agreement allowed the user of the building complete control and responsibility for the property. The only thing the lessee could not do was sell the building for a specified number of years. The lease would be for a nominal amount.

After viewing a number of buildings that did not fit the PRC/ DCC specifications, the "house hunters" were shown a one-story building on Roosevelt Road. The location was ideal and two access approaches to Roosevelt Road provided convenient parking and a suitable traffic pattern from a side street. All the other features Dorothy and Carol wanted were there. Dorothy then began work on the grant application. The mayor of Wheaton, Gwen Henry, was instrumental in making the building the property of the City of Wheaton. The grant was for $455,250 and the lease from the city was for $1.00 per year. The building, which had been the headquarters of the International Blind Mission, was unoccupied except for a caretaker, who lived in a small apartment in the rear. The caretaker was a member of a group calling itself "Peace Makers" and the PRC allowed this group to use the waiting room for its occasional meetings. The two miracles—finding a place and being able to pay for it—had happened as if on schedule.

Moving took place on New Year's Eve, 1992. The needed renovations started within days. Members of the IBEW electrical workers union brought the building up to code with donated labor, and a security system was donated. Bob Dwyer, an architect and a member of REC, coordinated the work and designed a conveyer belt to carry food down to the basement when it was delivered and to bring boxes of groceries up to clients for the Tuesday distribution. An engineer from Bell Labs brought some of his friends together and built shelving for food storage in the basement. Dorothy estimated that, all told, donated labor and equipment came to $19,000. This was yet another miracle because the total budget of the Center at the time was about $31,000. An open house was scheduled for the end of January 1993 but, in good PRC tradition, the event did not happen until March. By that time, some of the donors, all of the volunteers, and many of the clients had already been able to marvel at the amount of space that the PRC and the DCC now had for their use.

An unforeseen blessing of the new building was a good-sized open area that was separated from the waiting room but right next to the kitchen. One of the first spaces cleaned and renovated, this open area—with a large donated table—began to serve as a conference room for board meetings and a dining room for staff, volunteers, and visitors. The smell of food being prepared in the kitchen was soon the magnet that drew together members of the PRC and the DCC community. Volunteers, who had worked all of

Volunteers and staff of the PRC and DCC
celebrating the new larger home

Volunteers at Roosevelt Road food pantry. Every family received at least one pre-packaged box.

Tuesday morning in the often cold basement, making up boxes of groceries and heaving them on to the conveyer belt, especially welcomed the warmth of those sitting around the table and the invitation to "pick up some food in the kitchen and join us for lunch."

A vaguely foreseen, but nonetheless stressful, result of moving into the new building was a rapid increase in pantry use. In its first full year of operation, the Roosevelt Road location served 15,000 individuals, and sometimes as many as 500 different families a month. The sign, "SORRY, OUT OF FOOD TILL NEXT WEEK," had to be put up all too often. Al White was quoted as saying, "We sometimes saw as many people in a day as we saw the whole first year." Coffee and donuts were set out in the waiting room for those who had to wait. An experiment was tried in which volunteers gave informal parenting classes to those clients who had the time to stay a bit longer. The difficulty of trying to conduct a class in an open waiting room proved overwhelming and the idea was dropped. Volunteers doing intake also noticed that more of the clients were coming over longer periods of time. The original intention of providing short-term emergency help had given way to the fact that

Food distribution from the basement to the clients' cars.
Paper bags were used when boxes ran out.

some clients were becoming dependent on the food pantry. All of this increased usage was variously attributed to the better location and access of the new building as well as to higher long-term unemployment in a relatively weak economy.

In a letter to PRC sponsors written in the early 1990s, Dorothy gave donors a glimpse of the kind of people who were using the pantry:

- A well-educated middle-aged man who has lost his job due to corporate reorganization.
- A young married couple who both work to support their children.
- A single parent whose husband has left her and her two children.
- An elderly couple who rely on the pantry to supplement their Social Security income.

The new building was able to accommodate the influx of new clients, but donations were not keeping pace with demand. Dorothy began to ask pastors of individual churches to adopt the pantry for one Sunday a year. A number of churches responded with money, food, and even volunteers to shelve what they had brought in. Some pastors allowed Dorothy or one of the board members to speak to the congregation on a Sunday morning. Dorothy, Al White, and others were able to contact area schools. Al singled out Madison School in Wheaton for "bringing us food and clothing every month." Because of the increased demand on the pantry, Al was hired as a part-time employee after almost ten years as a volunteer.

An Attempt at Expansion

As Dorothy sat in her new office, still shared but with more space than she had had for eighteen years, she began work in 1993 on yet another change. West Chicago, just west of Wheaton, was the home of quite a few of the PRC's clients. Some of those clients liked the community atmosphere at the Center and asked Dorothy to set up something like it in their suburb. The Inland Properties division of the West Chicago Police Department donated a space in the Westwood Apartments and the West Chicago Human Services Center was opened in July 1993.

In order to establish this branch, Dorothy pledged $3,500 from the PRC. She was also able to get pledges for financial help from the DuPage Community Foundation, the Winfield Junior Women's Club, and the Hinsdale Center for the Arts. The total of pledged help came to $10,000. This meant that a substantial amount, over $34,000, had to be raised. The grant application Dorothy wrote to cover this amount included the following mission statement for the project:

The goals of the West Chicago/Westwood project are:

- to develop a sense of community/neighborhood that enhances the quality of life for the tenants and respects the unique talents and gifts of each individual in this culturally diverse population;
- to provide the resources to improve decision-making skills, elevate self-esteem and strengthen family relationships;
- to encourage cooperative efforts among tenants, manage-

ment, community groups, and churches to work for the mutual benefit of Westwood and for the West Chicago Community-at-large and to demonstrate that private–public partnerships can work toward the benefit of the whole community.

There is no mention and there was no intention of setting up another food pantry or clothes closet at the Westwood apartments. The programs suggested in the grant application included educational programs, peer tutoring, a job club, driver's education, and information on drugs and gangs. The recreational programs were arts/crafts and a summer day camp.

All of the above were to be funded by a total of $45,900, of which $10,000 was listed as in-kind and had already been pledged. The project was staffed by two administrators and an assistant. One of the administrators was a volunteer and a resident of Westwood, while the other came from the PRC. A West Chicago police officer maintained an "Officer Friendly" presence at Westwood. From its opening in July 1993, the new West Chicago Center offered English as a Second Language (ESL), tutoring, and recreational programs for children. These had been requested by the residents and at the start appeared to be successful.

By the end of 1993, however, interest in the new center had lessened among the residents of Westwood. The minutes of the PRC board meeting for March of 1994 noted that the resident administrator had quit and the PRC staff member was spending only five hours a week at Westwood. There is no indication of which, if any, of the programs was still in operation, but in July 1994 the PRC's participation in the West Chicago Human Services Center ceased and its operation was taken over by the Police Department. A detailed report on the closing of the PRC's first expansion venture was never issued, but Dorothy reached one conclusion that was to become an administrative principle: "Do not try to open up a major extension unless the PRC has complete administrative control of its operation."

A different kind of expansion, less public but still very important was the administration of Federal Emergency Management Assistance (FEMA) grants for housing. The PRC had been distributing FEMA money since 1982. Emergency Services Program

Grants were added later. These two programs helped individuals and families stay in their homes by providing rent or mortgage payments when there was danger of eviction. The aim was to prevent homelessness that for some clients was only one or two missed rent or mortgage payments away. The PRC cooperated with the housing division of the Department of Human Resources as well as with local agencies, Catholic Charities and the Salvation Army, to screen applicants and to disburse federal money to those in need. The expansion of this distribution of funds was dramatic, from $14,000 in 1982 to $132,000 just ten years later.

Dorothy's Death

In 1993, as part of the grant application for the West Chicago project, Dorothy wrote a summary of the PRC's accomplishments since its founding. Taken together, these accomplishments painted an impressive profile of an organization that had brought about significant changes in DuPage County.

- Operates a food pantry whose clients provide the leadership...to meet their needs.
- Wrote the original incorporation for the Family Shelter Service.
- A founding member of the Human Needs Coalition. Developed the DuPage P.A.D.S shelter program for the homeless.
- Cooperated with other agencies in establishing the DuPage Community Clinic.
- Received a Community Development Block Grant through the sponsorship of the city of Wheaton...to expand services to residents of DuPage County.
- Presently developing a facility in West Chicago.
- Expanded services to include an Adopt-a-Family Program and the Christmas "Share the Spirit" giving program. Operates a Clothes Closet for county residents in need.
- Administers FEMA emergency housing funds...to provide one month's rent or mortgage assistance to eligible households.

The list was formidable and one in which Dorothy took justifiable pride. In a letter she wrote in June 1993 to "Friends of the

People's Resource Center" she listed all of the above achievements and added that the PRC had received a grant from Apple Computer for an interagency communications network to link the PRC with other DuPage County social services. She commented, "We had been launched into the Age of Technology."

In the same letter, Dorothy illustrated the scope of her personal influence when she wrote that the DuPage County Health Department was able to find funding for prenatal care of low-income women with the cooperation of physicians and Loyola University Hospital.

This thumbnail history of the accomplishments might have been a sign that Dorothy finally felt settled in a place the PRC could call its own. However, there may be another explanation. Dorothy was then sixty-eight years old and feeling the effects of years that included her own large family and the activism that led to the founding of both the Peace and Justice Center and the PRC. She may have had thoughts of retiring despite the fact that she seemed to have as much energy as when she founded the Center. A still further indicator of her view of the future was the hiring of an assistant whom she appeared to be grooming to assume director-ship of the Center. Betsy Champaign began to work with Dorothy and to start the long process of understanding how the Center func-tioned and of meeting the many contacts Dorothy had made through the years. As 1993 ended and the Center celebrated its first anniversary in the new building, all programs of the PRC and the DCC were running smoothly. The number of clients coming for food, clothing, and medical care continued to increase and Doro-thy's job settled into a normal routine of fund-raising and overseeing the whole operation. It was in the summer of 1994 that she began feeling a bit unwell. Her first reaction was to say nothing and continue working. By late August, however, the pain was in-creasing and she was losing her normal vigor. She went to her doctor for medical tests and the results came back positive for liver cancer. In early September, she could not come to work. Her con-dition became rapidly worse and the news that everyone at the Center had feared came on September 28. The Center's founder and only executive director had died. Her funeral Mass at St. Jo-seph's Church in Downers Grove was crowded with her family and the many people she had come to know in the nineteen years of

Memorial celebrating the life of
Dorothy McIntyre, November 1994

the PRC's existence. Under a light rain Dorothy was buried with a
simple graveside ceremony at Queen of Heaven Cemetery in Hill-
side, Illinois.

"What happens now?" was the theme of many conversations as
the PRC opened again after a short closure for mourning. There
had been practically no time for Betsy to make a transition from assistant to director. Lyn Conway, the president of the PRC board
stepped in to help in the day-to-day running of the Center, but she
could not devote full time to the job. Other board members helped
Betsy make contact with the many people Dorothy had relied on as
donors and as influential friends in the county, but as the cob-
bled-together leadership tried to replace Dorothy's experience, the
economy was only slowly coming out of a downturn and pressure
continued mounting on the PRC for more help to its clients.

In August, the *Chicago Tribune* had run a story that mentioned the PRC.

> Economists are talking recovery with unemployment down
> and corporate earnings up. But it wasn't apparent to Jean P.,
> an unemployed single mother, with three children to feed and
> a run on food boxes at the People's Resource Center: "We are
> coming out of a recession. I want to know where and when."

Lyn shortly had to assume full leadership because Betsy Champaign's husband was relocated to Washington, D.C., and Betsy left her employment at the Center. One of Lyn's first acts as board of directors president was to get the board to begin a search for a new executive director. This was completely new territory for the PRC board because Dorothy's leadership had always been a given. Looking forward to a new person at the director's desk was a prospect to which no one had given serious thought. Fortunately for the PRC, its reputation was solid and qualified applicants were willing to submit résumés and take a chance on the People's Resource Center's future. In the meantime, however, funding began to diminish. The new occupant of the executive director's chair was going to face a lean start in the new job.

The months between Dorothy's death and the new executive director's arrival were filled with apprehension and soul-searching on the part of all involved with the PRC. Its two major programs, the Food Pantry and the Clothes Closet continued to operate, but funds for food purchases were in doubt. Donations of food continued but the pantry was increasingly dependent on food purchased from the Northern Illinois Food Bank and occasional direct purchases from Aldi. The Clothes Closet, though not dependent on purchased clothing, had already instituted a point system to limit clothing distribution so that the many who were seeking clothes could get a better choice.

Lyn continued on a part-time basis to handle some of the everyday work of acknowledging donations, paying bills, and meeting payroll. She had instituted the search for Dorothy's successor and had to screen applications that came in. It was then the board of directors came to realize that they were faced with a responsibility they were not prepared to handle. Through the nineteen years that Dorothy had led the PRC, the board of directors had been chosen by her from among her friends and had acted as a group of advisors who could be called upon to become involved in projects when help was necessary. This arrangement fit Dorothy's leadership style well because she was an energetic visionary who had a no-nonsense charisma that appealed to everyone who was interested in sharing the resources of DuPage County's residents. Her rapport with political leaders, foundations, and donors was legendary as were her interactions with her staff, volunteers, and clients. She was the go-to person whenever a need or problem arose in the organization and she was the innovator whenever anything new was begun at the Center. She saw the PRC as a movement whose organization could remain fluid under her direction. What she had not envisioned was an emergency succession plan...nor had the board.

Dorothy's death suddenly changed the leadership pattern, but the board of directors was not ready to take over the governance of the organization. The members did not consider themselves to be the governing body and it was only with the prospect of having to hire Dorothy's successor that their true role began to become clear. Going through the screening and hiring process was to be a learning experience for the board. The first revelation was that the new executive director would have to be paid. Dorothy's years of free service had created a kind of myth that anyone who wanted her job would likewise be a volunteer. Talking about a salary, especially a salary that a competent and experienced professional might expect seemed almost morally wrong. The second revelation followed from the hiring process. The new executive director was to be the employee of the board and would act according to the board's directives. It took a while for board members to understand that the new person would not be a clone of Dorothy, but rather a skilled professional who had experience in another organization where the board of directors *did* govern. It was this atmosphere that the new person would encounter and board members realized that they faced a new era in the evolution of the PRC.

As the slow process of the search went forward, staff and volunteers filled in as best they could. Donations continued to come in but total funding was down. Meanwhile, the food pantry was experiencing growing pains. In October 1994, Warren Roth, as a pantry volunteer as well as a board member, wrote a note to the board in response to the annual report:

The pantry has about reached its limit. This is the feeling of most of the people who work in it. With clients coming at the rate of more than 125 a week, Al White has been forced to tell some of those standing in line on Tuesday morning that they should not wait because we will not be able to serve them. Al has resorted to giving out only 125 numbers and even that limit requires filling 25 extra boxes each Tuesday as the distribution goes on.

Later in the year, "Share the Spirit" went on as usual and to all outward appearances, the People's Resource Center was functioning normally. Staff and volunteers were feeling both excitement and apprehension about the prospect of a new executive director. Carol McHaley and the staff and volunteers of the DuPage Community Clinic were also very interested in the new person coming to the PRC because, though legally separate, the two entities coexisted under one roof and issues such as space, utilities, and parking, were of mutual concern.

In February, the board conducted its final interviews and then announced that Mary Ellen Durbin (pictured below) would be the new executive director. Mary Ellen, who had held a similar position at Catholic Charities in Joliet, Illinois, had known Dorothy professionally and had admired the PRC for the community spirit Dorothy had been able to maintain as well as for its growth as an independent organization. Except for Rosie Dixon, no one on the board had known Mary Ellen

beforehand, but all were impressed by her résumé and her interview. When she formally took over the executive director's position, board members breathed a collective sigh of relief, feeling that they could once again relax and let her run the place as Dorothy had. Mary Ellen did not share that sentiment. Her idea was a working and engaged board with whom she could discuss present programs and future possibilities and then expect authoritative decisions and active participation in the PRC's activities. She expected the board to govern and give her directives, but she also wanted board members to respect her experience and draw on the expertise she brought to the Center. Her arrival would continue the community spirit of the past but would begin a new phase in how the PRC would operate.

5

Years of Growth, 1995–2005

New Beginning

MARY ELLEN DURBIN became the second executive director of the People's Resource Center on April 1, 1995. She had known the organization through her contacts with Dorothy McIntyre during the 1980s and 1990s and together they cofounded the Human Needs Coalition in 1983. Mary Ellen had served on the board of DuPage PADS (Public Action to Deliver Shelter), which the PRC had fostered, and the board of Family Shelter Service that had been founded by REC members under Dorothy's direction. She had also worked on the Campaign For Human Development, the source of the first grant to the PRC in the early 1980s. It was fitting then that one of her first acts as executive director was to dedicate the building that Dorothy had acquired as The Dorothy McIntyre Community Center.

Though Mary Ellen was hired in February of 1995, the death of her mother forced her to postpone her first day on the job. When she started work, she found that the finances of the Center were precarious. There had been no financial report to the board of directors at their January meeting and the 1995-96 annual report contained no financial data. What she was also to learn when she started work in April was that there had been a burglary of the office two days before her hiring and all the donor records had been stolen along with the computers. During her first days on the job, she discovered the kinds of miracles that were routinely expected at the PRC. With no donor base, she was trying to figure out how to make contact with the people who could get funding started again. Fran Meyer, a volunteer who had worked for Dorothy, walked into Mary Ellen's office and handed her three spiral notebooks in which she had hand copied the names and addresses of donors and the amounts of all donations that had come in over the years. The new executive director looked through those books and knew that she could start immediately to contact those who would help get the PRC on its feet financially. It was not till early May that Mary Ellen understood how big a miracle those notebooks were. It was then that she got a financial report showing a balance of only $30,000 in the bank.

Mary Ellen spent the morning of her first day on the job not at her desk but out in the parking lot meeting some of the clients who had come for food distribution. Among those waiting in line was a member of her parish whom she knew. She expected that he would be bitter at having to come for food, but she found that his reaction was thankfulness that the PRC was there. When she came back to her desk and began going over mail, she was greeted by Fran Holtzman with coffee and a sweet roll. The gesture from a long-time volunteer was one of many that began to make her feel like a valued member of the community and not just the boss. The next day, Mary Ellen attended her first board of directors meeting. Board president Lyn Conway came to the meeting with the agenda written on the back of an envelope. Bob Russo, a REC member, was attending his first meeting as a board member as was Andy Schlickman. Andy was present because his wife Sandee, while volunteering in the food pantry, had overheard Mary Ellen say that the PRC would need a lawyer. When Mary Ellen met Andy, she also heard about his daughter's invitation to the sponsors evening because of her $1.20 contribution to the Center.

One reason why Mary Ellen was talking about needing a lawyer was an unexpected tax bill for $10,000 that arrived shortly after she did. After the initial shock and some slightly panicked phone calls, she determined that the department of Housing and Urban Development (HUD) had not received all the necessary documentation on the PRC's tax-exempt status. Andy offered the services of lawyers from Sidley Austin for whom he worked. Working pro bono the lawyers found the paperwork mistake that had resulted in the tax bill. Their pro bono help in numerous legal matters has continued to be a steady support for the PRC.

The eight months since Dorothy's death had been a rough patch and it did not take the new director long to find out that she had an uphill climb to get the organization on a solid footing once again. But the warm welcome she had received from everyone on her first day of work, including the illuminated sign in the front of the building, which read "Mary Ellen Is Here," had convinced her that she had come to the place where, in her own words, "she really wanted to be." As she settled in, the new executive director became familiar with the organization by handling crises and launching initiatives that led to its steady growth.

Housing

Housing problems in DuPage County had not been unknown to REC members when they brought the People's Resource Center into existence. Among REC's first members were Charles and Jan Tyler, an interracial couple who recounted their own difficulties buying a house in Downers Grove. At an early REC meeting Charles and Jan described how they had been told at more than one real estate office that nothing was available despite the fact that they had no financial problems. Others, for whom race was not an issue, were considered "low income" and their story was much the same. Little or nothing was available because houses were expensive and moderate-rent apartments were practically nonexistent. Working with the Franciscan Sisters in Wheaton, REC members were involved in the development of Marian Park, the first low- and medium-income apartments in the County, on the property owned by the Sisters.

Other REC members played important roles in addressing the inequalities in the DuPage housing market. Ruth Riha and Phil Chinn helped in the founding of H.O.P.E. (Homes of Private Enterprise) with Bernie Kleina. Later, in the early 1990s, Dick and Florence Nogaj established the DuPage branch of Habitat for Humanity. Both of these organizations aimed to bring affordable housing to DuPage residents; both ran into opposition.

Another kind of problem faced the PRC soon after Mary Ellen arrived. The PRC's 1995 annual report provides the following account:

> After 12 years of receiving FEMA funds to assist economi-
> cally distressed families with rent and mortgage assistance,
> DuPage County did not meet the FEMA formula. The for-
> mula used to determine eligibility for FEMA funds is based
> on the percentage rate of unemployment and/or poverty. The
> loss of FEMA funds represented a loss of $267,000 in direct
> funds available to county residents in financial trouble and
> $156,000 in rent and mortgage assistance. The PRC had ad-
> ministered these funds for Catholic Charities, the DuPage
> County Housing Resource Department, and the Salvation
> Army and it represented a major part of the safety net to keep
> people from becoming homeless. The irony is that the raw
> numbers in poverty continued to increase, but with the tremen-
> dous population growth spurt in the county, the percentage of
> people in poverty has actually decreased.

The loss of FEMA funds was a blow to the agencies involved in
providing shelter and preventing homelessness. As an already ac-
knowledged leader in DuPage and Will counties, Mary Ellen was
asked to attend a meeting in Washington, D.C., to discuss with representatives from FEMA a modification of its formula. She could
not, however, get the funds restored that DuPage County had lost
and so when she returned to Illinois, she made an application for
State funds to partially offset the loss of FEMA money.

Later in 1995, federal money again began coming to the county
when HUD awarded $1.8 million to the county for transitional
housing and "intensive services on behalf of multi-problem homeless families." The award went to the DuPage County Housing
Authority, but the PRC provided the coordination function. The
initial loss had been reversed, Mary Ellen had become known for
her advocacy, and the PRC had once more become an important
player in the fight against homelessness. Work with the homeless
became even more focused when Linda Cheatham was hired in
1996 to administer the HUD program called "Supportive Housing
Initiative for Families in Transition" (SHIFT). This program
aimed to maximize the resources of a number of agencies and min-
imize duplication of effort. Providing a comprehensive transitional
housing program for families with multiple and acute problems

was another of its goals. Linda was able to respond to more than 1,700 homeless and at-risk callers. Almost 1,200 of these callers were assessed and given referrals to transitional housing in DuPage County. As with hunger and medical care, very few county officials wanted to believe that there was homelessness on that scale in DuPage. By 1998, however, the SHIFT program was turned over to the county's Human Services Division and the PRC provided the training program for county employees. The PRC maintained contact with sixteen multiple-needs families and provided them various forms of assistance including monetary help.

Providing for the homeless in the mid 1990s was part of the PRC's growth, but was not a totally new service component of the organization. As early as 1983, Dorothy had involved the PRC in the DuPage Homeless Prevention Partnership by acting as a facilitator in the effort to bring small and scattered groups together to assess and act on a growing problem in the county. Then in 1985, with the help of the Human Needs Coalition, Dorothy hired Barbara Brent to be director of DuPage PADS. This effort was modeled on a program developed in Aurora by Hesed House. The program was to find churches to provide emergency housing for those who were in need of shelter on any given day. Starting with St. Mary's Church in Downers Grove, the new program offered homeless persons an evening meal, cots for sleeping, and breakfast. Volunteers from the church took over the job of preparing meals, setting out bedding, and cleaning up the following day. Other churches became involved and DuPage PADS became an emergency shelter that meant survival when the weather became life threatening. In 1989, DuPage PADS was incorporated as a separate nonprofit entity and was spun off from the PRC.

As DuPage PADS solved emergency needs, Dorothy recognized the needs of people who were in danger of losing their homes. She started a transitional housing program that was at first a part of DuPage PADS and then became a separate program within the PRC after 1989. This program continues to be active and was joined in 2000 by the DuPage Housing Action Coalition (DHAC), an advocacy group that worked to make local, state, and federal officials more aware of the county's special needs for affordable housing. As in every other service the PRC provided, addressing one problem led to finding another. Mary Ellen, with her experience from Catholic Charities, was no stranger to the process of uncovering problems. Like Dorothy, she addressed new problems by bringing together people and organizations to provide a county-wide approach to solutions.

Once SHIFT was no longer coordinated at the PRC, Linda Cheatham was able to devote her time to the Center's finance problems. She and Mary Ellen worked together to get the organization onto a sound business footing. Linda bought a software accounting system and she and Mary Ellen organized fund-raising through grants, the existing donor base, and special events. Since not-for-profits were subject to government audits, Linda arranged the accounts in order and began working on human resources, an area that had little formal consideration under Dorothy's administration. Between Mary Ellen and Linda, the PRC began to arrive at a business model that allowed it to function smoothly and without the financial ups and downs it had experienced after Dorothy's death. As the PRC grew and more paid staff were hired, Linda developed the management system needed to make the hiring process formal and appropriate for a not-for-profit organization. Mary Ellen brought this new model to the board and board members came to the realization that their responsibilities would now go well beyond discussing problems and making suggestions.

Dental Clinic

As early as 1989, the dental health of clients was a topic of discussion among the staff of the newly formed DuPage Community Clinic. Dorothy had begun informal talks with county Health Department officials about the possibility of a free dental clinic. Dental needs of clients coming for medical care had become obvious during examinations, and the answer to questions about seeing a dentist were always the same; "We have no money." The county did have a Dental Care Referral Program but only nine dentists in the county accepted these referrals and there was still a small fee for services. Many were also referred to the Loyola Dental School, but when that facility closed no free dental care was available for the very poor.

Discussion focused the problem, but finding a solution was another matter. The PRC was still in the house on Indiana Avenue and it was bursting at the seams with the programs that already existed there. Finding space for a program as complex as a dental clinic seemed out of the question. Dorothy and Carol knew that they could arouse interest and get funds, but they could not create more space. The Dental Clinic remained in the talking stage until the move to the new building on Roosevelt Road. The former care-taker's apartment provided the room and with this space, the rest was doable.

As when other problems were perceived at the PRC, Dorothy relied on miracles, but she also wrote grant proposals. One Com-munity Development Block Grant had allowed the PRC to get a new home, and a second CDBG brought the dental clinic to reality. The grant, which was for $96,500, was awarded in 1993. An advi-sory board had to be formed because the configuration of the space into operatories was a job for dental professionals. The remodeling contract was let out for bids and members of the advisory board so-licited donated equipment for three operatories. Dorothy's death in 1994 intervened to slow the process, but by November 1995 work began. The work was slowed considerably when asbestos was found and its removal required sealing off both the apartment and part of the basement that housed the food pantry. The members of the advisory board had to revamp their budget and the final cost for the renovation and installation of equipment came to $138,000. The PRC had to absorb the additional cost.

In July 1995, Medicaid payments for adult dental care were ter-minated. This gave the advisory board an additional incentive to get the dental clinic into operation because it was to become the only free adult dental care available in DuPage County. The board had already enlisted four dentists who would volunteer time to work in the clinic and they had solid promises of $46,000 worth of donated equipment and supplies. Pat Sieben was chosen as the di-rector of the new program; the first patients began to be treated in 1996. Pat brought in volunteer hygienists and she coordinated the schedules of volunteer dentists with appointments of clients. The program represented a major cooperative endeavor involving an ongoing partnership between business and educational, govern-mental, health and human service entities, including the Dental Care Program of the DuPage County Health Department and the West Suburban Branch of the Chicago Dental Society. The Chi-cago Dental Society provided the PRC board of directors with a new member, Dr. Keith Suchy, a practicing dentist and president of the Society. The board, with Keith, who later became its president, was thus able to make decisions relating to the Dental Clinic based on expert advice.

When it began operation in 1996, the Dental Clinic was able to open only one day a week. It provided basic primary dental care, including an initial examination, necessary x-rays, cleaning/hygiene education, simple fillings, nonsurgical extractions, basic screening, information and education, referral, and linkage to needed resources. Complex procedures were referred to volunteer dentists at their own offices. In emergency cases, pain relief was provided before a referral was made. The Dental Clinic did not offer orthodontics, oral surgery, or procedures involving the use of nitrous oxide.

Two years later, the program had hired an assistant director and was open four days a week and still staffed with only volunteer dentists and hygienists.

In 1999, the Dental Clinic expanded its services into a "Total Treatment Plan" and a "Holistic Oral Family Health Practice." Then, in early 2001, the clinic was spun off from the PRC and merged with the DuPage Community Clinic, thus creating a comprehensive health care program in one building and under the administration of the DCC. Pat Sieben and three dental assistants became employees of the DCC, thus making the transition smooth and complete. By the time the dental clinic was turned over to DCC, it had served 2,054 DuPage residents, most of whom had come to the PRC originally as clients for other services.

As Mary Ellen looked over the lists of clients in all its programs in 1996, she drew up a sketch of the people who were coming to the Center, borrowing from a song that had recently become popular.

We discovered that *We Are the World*. The PRC serves people from forty-seven different countries of origin. *We Are the Children*. Half of the people we serve are children. *We Are Working*. More than half of the guests are employed but still have to use a food pantry. And *We Are a Community of Volunteers*, supported by a very small staff, 30 percent of our volunteers started with us as guests, in need of our services.

She would look over those client lists many times and find that both the number of clients and the number of countries represented continued to increase. Her conclusion was the same as Dorothy's had been, "We need more space."

Moving Again

With the Dental Clinic in operation, the PRC was once again experiencing the old problem, too little space for its programs. New programs in their early stages—art, literacy, and computer training—had to function outside the Roosevelt Road building.

In 1999, Mary Ellen asked the board for authorization to seek a larger building. The board started a capital campaign and the search was on. Together with a committee including George Carr and board member Bob Russo, Mary Ellen started looking at buildings that had the room and the configuration the PRC needed. Progress was slow because just the right building had to be in a part of DuPage County that was easily reached by clients.

In June 2003, the PRC closed on a two-story office building at the north end of Naperville Road, only a short distance from downtown Wheaton. After needed remodeling was completed, the PRC moved into its third home in March 2005. Program expansion was now possible. One example of expansion in the food program was the introduction of choice, that is, the use of food carts by clients. This was one of the first initiatives of Melissa Travis when she took over the directorship the Food Pantry, the Clothes Closet, Homeless Prevention, and "Share the Spirit." Program expansion, at the turn of the new millennium, was not limited to the new building in Wheaton. As the number of clients coming from the southeastern part of DuPage County increased, Mary Ellen proposed to the board an expansion into Westmont. In 2001, a pantry was opened in the Alliance Church on Cass Avenue, but within a few years, the demand for food made a larger facility necessary. In 2008, the pantry moved into a rented space that allowed also for the empowerment programs, art, literacy, and computer training, and job assistance to be offered there.

6

Into the New Millennium

New Direction—Empowerment

THE HISTORY OF THE PEOPLE'S RESOURCE CENTER was a constant struggle to supply the means of survival for its clients. However, when food, clothing, shelter, and medical care were provided, other needs became obvious. Staff and volunteers recognized that clients needed more for fulfillment and self-sufficiency. Once recognized, these needs led to the development of innovative programs in art, literacy, computer training, and job training. Though started in the 1990s, these programs grew rapidly as the new millennium began.

Women's Wisdom Art Program

As the PRC returned to a sound financial footing after 1995, the new executive director looked for growth and found it being delivered to her doorstep. REC member Nancy Castle developed an idea she heard about from a friend in California. In her own words:

> It was the summer of 1996 and I was still fairly new to REC.... We had each been asked to take responsibility for a liturgy. As my week approached and I wondered what I would do, my answer came in the mail. A friend in California had been working with homeless women for years, and was dismayed by the rate of recidivism—it seemed

64

the women could not manage their lives to maintain the goods and facilities provided to them. Laura Ann, being an artist at heart, decided that the creativity nurtured when doing artwork might give them the inner strength and confidence to care for themselves. Excited with her success, she sent a summary of the program she had devised, and examples of the results, to a group of friends, including me. I thought the idea of doing art together in a supportive community environment, and realizing our own personal growth through that process, would be a wonderful experience for me and many other women. Voila! Here was my liturgy ready-made! When I read and described the report on Sunday everyone was enthusiastic, saying we should have a program like that at the PRC.

In 1996, Rosie Dixon, another REC member, accompanied Nancy to Sacramento, California, to look at an art program for women. Barb Brent, as director of DuPage PADS, went with them with the intention of starting her own art program. Nancy continues her account:

Co-founders of Women's Wisdom Art Program
Nancy Castle (left) and Rosie Dixon (right), with
long-time volunteer and artist Mary Hamlin

We spent a full day participating in the classes, talking with the participants and viewing the art on display. We accepted their goals and philosophy and used them as our beginning framework. The most salient were: (1) everyone is a participant (you can't just sit and watch); (2) everyone is equal (in the sense of personal dignity—just like the PRC); (3) everyone is inherently creative.

In the fall of 1997, Rosie, Nancy, and Kathy Johnson started Women's Wisdom, a community of artists and writers. Like most programs, this one had its nomadic years. The first few months were spent in the basement of the Wheaton Franciscan Sisters Convent because the program needed a considerable amount of space and decisions had not yet been made on allocating that space at the PRC. At the convent, all supplies had to be carried through the building and down to the basement, and then removed at the end of the two-hour session. When the program moved into the PRC's Clothes Closet at the more accessible Roosevelt Road location, many more were able to take part in the Women's Wisdom program. But the new space-sharing arrangement proved to be inconvenient for those trying to maintain normal operations in the Clothes Closet. Plus, there was always the fear that a client would mistake the coat of a Women's Wisdom participant for one ready to be distributed by the Clothes Closet. On the plus side, however, the two programs being in the same location meant that clients were discovering and becoming interested in Women's Wisdom courses. After a short stay in the Clothes Closet, the art program moved into a rented space, called the Enrichment Center, a small storefront on Lorraine Avenue about a block away from PRC's building. This Enrichment Center was also shared with the ESL program and the computer program, both of which had recently started. It was only later, after the PRC had moved to the Naperville Road address, that Women's Wisdom was given two permanent rooms and a study/pottery kiln room.

Nancy Castle and Rosie Dixon, codirectors of Women's Wisdom in 2005, reflected on the development of the program in *Women's Wisdom Quarterly*, a publication they had started:

We are an art community—that is what we have become, a community, strong in regard to its members yet open and welcoming to newcomers. Women from all walks of life come here, women who are poor and some who are not so poor, women who have been scarred by life's battles and some who have come through relatively unscathed. We come together every week, with respect for one another and great good humor. Our studio is a safe, comforting place for laughing, experimenting, telling our stories or keeping our silence, and making incredible art and poetry.

Expressed as policies, these thoughts became:

Women's Wisdom intends to provide a safe, caring, and supportive environment. In class it is important that we all treat each other with respect and tolerance, and appreciate each other's boundaries. Women's Wisdom classes are designed particularly for adult women. In the future we may be planning special mother and daughter or co-ed classes.

The Art and Writing section of the first issue of *Women's Wisdom Quarterly* featured a poem in which nine women addressed the question, "What would you change?"

Eve's Wisdom

"I would change salaries."
"I would change my grandson's decision to join the Marines."
"I would change the weeds in my garden to roses."
"I would change igneous hearts back into lava."
"We would see God more clearly."
"No more war, no more homelessness or unemployment."
"We would start out looking old and grow younger."
"I would change the world's underwear every day."
"We will learn to forgive our mistakes."

When Nancy retired as codirector in 2005 Rosie became the sole director of Women's Wisdom until she herself retired in 2008. Nancy reminisced about her time at the PRC:

I was very lucky to find others who wanted to make it happen at the PRC and to be codirector for the beginning years. It makes me happy to see how this program brings strength and healing to the participants—and how that gets passed along to everyone at the PRC.

An early student at Women's Wisdom, Louise Schuster, echoed some of the same thoughts: "When I first came, I just felt so accepted. Everybody is accepted here. We're all considered equal here, even if you have no talent at all." Rosie recalled another early student, Pam Gallagher:

Pam Gallaher was one of our first women. She had come to the PRC over on Indiana, as a single mother who had left an abusive situation—with five sons, which included triplets. Pam went on to be one of the first people to get a house through DuPage Homeownership Center. Pam is a poster woman for PRC. She brought up her boys, went to COD, got a job, kept her house and is now retired. She still comes to the writing group at WW. She always credits us with keeping her sane while she was going through so much.

In 1999, the youngest member of the group, Nicki, created a Christmas card that was put up for sale. The theme, "Street Angel," came directly from her own experience. Besides providing sales opportunities for its participants, Women's Wisdom branched out. In 1998, an outreach program was started at Family Shelter Service. Though it lasted only two years, the program was a forerunner of a larger expansion that would come later.

Rosie recounted a pottery story from the Family Art Program:

I came in one morning and found one of the women, who is also a computer instructor, working on her piece. I admired it and asked when she did it. She said, "Friday night." I said, "We don't have any class on Friday night, the building is closed." She said, "Oh, I have a key. It's girl's night out and there are so many women who love pottery that we need another night to work. Sometimes we stay till almost midnight." This woman is a computer whiz. I told her that we would have to stop the class until we got permission from the director. Of course, we never did.

Another pottery class was taught by Ben Calvert. Ben innovated within the program because he welcomed and tried to recruit men into his class. Few men came, but the women kept the attendance high and they were impressed by his kindness and patience with them. They produced a wide variety of pottery pieces and at the

2006 show, held at "Goddesses in the Garden," every piece sold.
Rosie Dixon summed up an unexpected result she observed in the first years of the program:

> I am surprised by how "spiritual" we were when we started. Every meeting was begun by a reading—maybe a candle lighting and some kind of reference to the strength of women. Maybe we were trying to be too therapeutic. Anyway, it sort of brought tears to my eyes. We were so engaged in what we were doing—not just art but a life-changing scenario.

Expansion of the Art Program

Shortly after the PRC's move to the Naperville Road location, a pottery class and a writing program started with Sarah Crago. In 2006, Community Art Partners for Kids at Risk began independently of the PRC in order to provide after-school programs. The People's Resource Center later absorbed this initiative and the Kids Art Program came into existence. The Kids Art Program allowed the PRC to partner with neighborhood resource centers at a variety of county locations, such as apartment complexes and in grade and middle schools. Established organizations, including World Relief and Outreach Ministries of the Village of Carol Stream, also provided locations for the program. The idea of locating temporary facilities all over the county solved the problem of space allocation at the Center and also allowed more children to participate because transportation to Wheaton was not necessary. The PRC recruited all the volunteer teachers and provided materials, while the people at each site recruited the children. With funding from corporations like Target, Staples, the Topfer Foundation, and the Naperville Rotary Club, the Kids Art Program grew to reach 500 children at thirteen locations and has been able to function successfully over the long term.

One variation on Kids Art was the Family Art Program, which began with sessions on Saturday mornings so as to involve adults and children together.

A Kids Art teacher at Woodridge Resource Center recalled one notable success that stemmed from the program's stability. A boy in her class was disruptive and refused to participate. Rather than ask him to leave, she enlisted him as her helper with special jobs each week. When he began to take part in the art program, she was able to find out the reason for his initial hostility. He liked the program but he was afraid that the classes would not continue and he would be judged a failure. As the weeks passed, the teacher found she had a dedicated student who had also overcome his lack of self-confidence.

When Lesley Gena succeeded Rosie Dixon as director of Women's Wisdom, she knew that an important part of her job was going to be recruiting volunteer art instructors for the program's many locations. She found the recruiting task was not very difficult, in part because she experienced one of the PRC minor miracles. A long-term art teacher from Downers Grove died suddenly, and the very next day Lesley received a call from a woman in the same suburb who wanted to know more about the program and to volunteer. Where miracles were not immediately forthcoming, the PRC website helped to match those interested in participating with program needs in specific areas of the county.

Shortly after she arrived in 2008, Lesley added more dimensions to the already formidable program. She initiated a sewing class, a dance class for kids, and a specialty group for watercolor painting. Meanwhile, the original Women's Wisdom group continued doing well selling its works. Lesley was also able to contact other local artists as guest experts for charcoal, pastels, and oil painting. The sewing class combined the artistic with the practical. One of the clients had a job interview scheduled, but did not have a jacket to go with her dress. She joined the sewing class and was able to make a jacket, with the PRC providing fabric, sewing materials, and a crash course in tailoring.

Dance classes provided another example of community involvement. After two classes at the Center proved that the space available there was inadequate for the interest the classes generated, Gary United Methodist Church of Wheaton offered its facilities, and the classes were able to continue. The classes in watercolors, on the other hand, were able to use the space at the Center and they were enhanced by the workshops given by nationally recognized watercolor artist Ratindra Das.

In 2010, a team from the Literacy, Job Assistance, and Art programs was formed by Barbara Tartaglione, a long-term volunteer and later the PRC's board president. The team's goal was to create opportunities for paid employment for women who were unable to work outside of their homes due to limited language ability, transportation, or child-care resources. A select group of eight clients was taught how to make jewelry by Betty James, a professional jewelry maker, who owned the Genuine Article, a bead shop in downtown Wheaton. The women took classes for several weeks to learn how to make handmade clay beads and jewelry. Lesley and Barbara taught the group the basic fundamentals of business ownership such as obtaining a business license through the county, designing and purchasing business cards, pricing and selling their products, and providing customer service at various sales within the community. This was the PRC's first venture in forming a social enterprise, with the goal of teaching clients how to start and manage a small home-based business.

Sales were conducted at churches and art fairs, as well as in home shows. The home venues proved to be the most productive sales vehicle for the group. Several of the artisans were very successful, and the additional income enabled them to add to their household's earnings for needs such as college textbooks. The pride and self-confidence from making beautiful products and having others purchase them was an important result of the program. Volunteer Liz Schrimmel photographed the jewelry for display on a website that volunteer Fran Strebendt created. This enabled each artisan to have her own product page with a bio and examples of her work and unique style. These styles reflected their various points of origin, including Sudan, Peru, and Mexico, as well as native Chicagoans. A second group of artisans was formed in 2011, with experienced participants from the previous year doing the instructing.

In addition to jewelry sales, art classes have extended their community outreach with exhibits of painting, watercolors, and collages in the Wheaton Community Center, Gallery 200 in West Chicago, Mercy Provena McAuley Manor, Carol Stream Public Library, Hope Presbyterian Church in Wheaton, The DuPage Framing Center, and the Theosophical Society, also in Wheaton. Trinity Episcopal Church has provided facilities for an exhibition on a yearly basis.

In 2009, Lesley was also able to start several classes at the newly established PRC Southeast in Westmont. A volunteer, Margaret Miranda, started teaching drawing and painting to classes that averaged seven participants. The works they produced were exhibited in 2010 at Great American Bagel in Westmont. The following year, PRC Southeast offered a six-week adult workshop called "Outside the Lines." This venture was experimental and gave students the opportunity to produce art pieces from different kinds of materials such as fabric, wire, and wood. The experiment proved successful enough that Lesley decided to offer a seven-week art class for senior citizens living at Marian Park in Wheaton.

As of 2011, all of the classes and workshops of the Art Program have served about 300 students each year. Lesley Gena coordinates the Art Program with the assistance of thirty volunteers in many locations around DuPage County. Carrying on and expanding the vision of Rosie Dixon and Nancy Castle, Lesley has established a program that gives clients and others an outlet for artistic expression at little or no cost to the participants. For many of the students not only has artistic ability been discovered, but more importantly, self-esteem has been enhanced. Though Dorothy never envisaged an Art Program for the PRC she founded, it is safe to say that she would have been enthusiastic about the results the program has produced.

Adult and Family Literacy

Soon after Mary Ellen became the PRC's executive director in 1995, she was chatting one day with food pantry clients waiting in line and realized that many of the clients did not speak English well. They were from Southeast Asia, Eastern Europe, Africa, Mexico, and elsewhere in Latin America. She decided that the PRC had to offer English as a second language if these immigrants were to succeed in the United States. Bringing that decision to reality, however, took longer than she expected: two years.

Her first step was to contact those agencies that were already offering ESL (English as a Second Language) classes. One person she contacted, Dr. Joanna Escobar at College of DuPage, encouraged her to create a "literacy pathway" for clients. She suggested further that the PRC and COD partner to establish a Family Literacy Program in West Chicago to help non–English-speaking parents and their children who were enrolled in Head Start programs. The meetings that followed involved staff from COD, Head

Start, and St. Mary's parish in West Chicago. The Literacy Program was to become a major effort in partnering.

Since it began in 1995, the adult and family literacy program has developed into individualized education for adults and children, including instruction in ESL, math, reading, writing, and citizenship. Tutoring has been done in an open classroom setting and on a one-to-one basis in many locations all over the county. At the same time Spanish-langugage conversation classes were initiated for PRC staff and volunteers. The program has also generated a book club and has taken on summer science classes for children.

The Adult and Family Literacy program is a good example of an initiative that emerged from one of the principles on which the original REC community was founded, "If you see a problem, you are anointed to address it."

Partnering

DuPage County agencies and institutions interested in promoting family literacy and strengthening family cohesiveness within Hispanic families in West Chicago formed a partnership that included the PRC, the West Chicago Public Library, LifeLink/Head Start, and the College of DuPage. Their first action was to collaborate on an application for funding submitted to the Illinois Secretary of State to develop a Family Literacy Program. The application was funded and a social worker, Geri Jender, was hired to establish the program, called "Leer es Poder" (Reading is Power). The program's goal, besides increasing literacy, was to build relationship skills among twenty Hispanic families with preschool children, sixty people in all. Leer es Poder stressed developmental growth, self-esteem, and family cohesiveness while reinforcing literacy in Spanish, English language skills, and knowledge of North American customs. The participants learned skills in using the library, engaged in parent-child learning activities, and, at the same time, developed a shared sense of community.

The PRC coordinated this partnership and handled recruitment, books, and transportation for families when these services were needed. Beyond these basics, the partnership provided assessment of individual and family literacy needs, separate adult and child literacy classes, intergenerational enrichment activities, and parent–child activities that promoted the transfer of what had been learned either at home or in class. All of this was supplemented with field trips, library experiences, community meals, and counseling to support self-esteem and family interaction. One outcome of the program was a 150 percent increase in West Chicago library use by the families in the program. From its inception, "Leer es Poder" relied on volunteers to provide one-on-one tutoring for language skills and babysitting services when needed. In order to maintain all of these functions, the PRC applied for and received a grant from the Campaign for Human Development.

Leer es Poder was effective for Hispanic families in West Chicago, but it did not meet the needs of the majority of non-English speaking clients who came from non-Latin countries. In 1999, the program was turned over to the College of DuPage. Using the West Chicago experience as a model, the PRC then initiated its own literacy program especially for the immigrants and refugees among its internationally diverse clientele, who by then represented more than one hundred countries. Barb Dorgan, an experienced adult literacy teacher, took over the program and began to meet with the Sisters of St. Joseph of La Grange. The Sisters had a "School on Wheels" program that offered ESL to adults in a former bookmobile. For about a year, the Literacy Program partnered with the Sisters' director of ministerial effectiveness, Barbara Bernhard, who brought the School on Wheels Bus to the PRC parking lot on food distribution days. This allowed food pantry clients easy access to the literacy program. The partnership also allowed Sr. Mary Beth McDermott to provide assistance in recruiting and training volunteers. The PRC then expanded the program with one-on-one tutoring in its Enrichment Center. Pam Knight was hired to coordinate the expanded Literacy Program. Staff at College of DuPage helped Pam get started and then provided teachers for the classes at the Enrichment Center. These cooperative initiatives improved the outreach of the PRC with its growing non– English-speaking adult clients and cemented a long-term relationship between the PRC and COD.

When Pam became the program's director in 1999, the Literacy Program was still in its infancy and had only six tutors and two partnerships in operation. As early as 1998, St. Joseph's Orthodox Church in Wheaton had a literacy program of its own. When the church joined its program with the PRC's, the number of volunteer tutors increased and students and tutors had more room to meet. The spirit of their program was to provide a family-like atmosphere; their motto was, "There is always room for one more student and one more teacher with a heart." This matched the spirit at the PRC perfectly and facilitated the later melding of the two programs (see below).

By 2001, the Family Literacy Program had expanded to include fifty-six families, with libraries, churches, service organizations, and mosques providing instruction space. The link between English proficiency and better employment was in the forefront of the program's goals. One-to-one tutoring continued to be the basic method used and recruiting tutors was one of the main activities of the Literacy Program's staff.

In 2005, when the PRC moved to its new location on Naperville Road, St. Joseph's Orthodox Church was only a block away. Circumstances had forced St. Joseph's to end its literacy program, but students were now able to come to the PRC. Some of the volunteers, like John Argyrakis, who had been volunteering at the church since 2001, continued at the new location.

As partnering fostered more outreach, LifeLink/Head Start once again joined the program, starting first in Wheaton in 2001

Pam Knight (left) of the PRC, Joy Aaronson (right)
of the Community Partnership for Head Start,
and women and children in the program

and then in Addison in 2007. Besides instruction in English and basic computer skills, this program was able to provide transportation, child care, and instructional materials for its clients' parents. Over the years, the number of Head Start parents served by the ESL program increased steadily in both locations.

An example of the need for literacy classes was seen on a Sunday morning in St. Isidore's Church in Bloomingdale. The pastor announced after a mass that the church would offer free ESL courses; forty-five people signed up immediately. According to the first coordinators in the parish, Lisa and Rich Muegge, "offering English tutoring to the parishioners at their church helps with their fears and apprehensions—and it's a nonthreatening situation." Tutors at St. Isidore's came from a wide variety of backgrounds. Margaret Roth, recently retired from Benedictine University, was having lunch with a colleague, Larry Kamin, and in the course of their conversation, Larry, a biology professor, mentioned that he was an ESL tutor at St. Isidore's. Another former professor, Luciano Rodriguez, had immigrated from Puerto Rico and found work as a software engineer. He volunteered first in the Computer Literacy Program, but soon realized that many of his Spanish-speaking students knew little English because of inadequate earlier schooling. He developed intensive classes that merged computer training, GED (General Education Development) preparation, and English. He held two-and-a-half-hour classes on Saturday mornings for the convenience of those students who were working. The classes included discussions of current events. Luciano also had students find American states on maps and then search on the internet for more information; they thus developed their reading skills while they looked up more information. The *Chicago Tribune Magazine* of January 23, 2005, quoted Luciano: "You can get depressed because behind every student there is a very bad life. Some work three jobs, some have abusive spouses, others have been swindled." After reading this article, a woman who worked for the Illinois Literacy Foundation nominated the PRC Literacy Program to receive donations from a Borders bookstore partnership. The Literacy Program continued to receive these donations for five years. Luciano never let the depressing situations of his students slow his work. He continued his computer and GED instruction and later served on the board of the People's Resource Center.

In 2012, Luciano won the "Governor's Volunteer Service Award" for 2012 for the northeastern Illinois region. The literacy staff had nominated him for "outstanding work as a computer instructor and literacy tutor, including co-ordination of classes such as computer instruction in Spanish, GED and financial literacy."

A further example of meeting the unique needs of adults in ESL, was the Saturday morning classes that Patricia Bernhold offered. Patricia recognized that many ESL students did not have sufficient opportunities to practice speaking English with others. She began to teach an intermediate-advanced English conversation class. Her impression of her class was that she was presiding over a mini United Nations gathered around a table sharing stories, practicing new vocabulary, and celebrating events of their own lives. Over the years, she has had contact with more than 130 students from around the world. Clients of the Literacy Program provide some of the best examples of what the program and its partners were able to accomplish:

- An East African woman who was raised in a refugee camp in Sudan was able to come to the United States with her husband and children. Though all her children succeeded in high school and some in college, her English was just functional until she started ESL classes at College of DuPage and tutoring classes at the PRC. While raising her children and working part-time on a night shift, she improved her mastery of English to the point that she was able to become a U.S. citizen. With only one year of formal schooling before coming to the United States, she was able, through ESL, to begin working on her GED.

- A single mother who had lost her job because of downsizing, came to the PRC for food. Though a graduate of a Chicago Public School, she was barely literate because of dyslexia. After she recognized her dyslexia—when her son was found to have the same condition—she contacted the Literacy Program and began working with a volunteer to improve her reading, writing, and spelling. She has also improved her oral communication skills through extensive weekly chats with her mentor.

Volunteer Bob Russo helps the Toto family
from Sudan study for their citizenship test

— A 57-year-old man, another victim of downsizing, lost his
job as a factory supervisor when his factory was sold.
Lacking a high school diploma he began working on a
GED in order to improve his chances of finding another
job.

Many who wished to take advantage of the Literacy Program
faced a problem of transportation. Without cars, getting to the
Center was difficult, because public transportation is limited in
DuPage County. Through its partnering with churches, community centers, and libraries, and with teachers from the College of
DuPage, the PRC was able to set up twenty-one neighborhood
sites for clients to meet with tutors. Still some of those who came to
these locations had to make extraordinary efforts to get there.

— A young man studying for his GED made the twenty-mile
round-trip from Hanover Park on his bicycle.

— In 2003, the daughter of a refugee contacted the PRC because her mother wanted to learn English and she and her
siblings in high school needed help in math. Since they
had no transportation a volunteer arranged to meet them at

a local library. Still, the library was a distance from their home. The whole family of five walked for an hour in the summer's heat to meet their tutor. The family was no stranger to difficulties. The father had been killed by a Russian missile in Afghanistan and while they were in a refugee camp in Pakistan their oldest son disappeared. When the family came to the United States, the woman had to communicate with landlords, teachers, dentists, doctors, sales clerks, and repairmen through her children. Thus the original need for her to learn English.

- A young mother who was a refugee from Sudan wanted to improve her English reading skill to help her children with their school work. Since she had no transportation to attend classes in Wheaton, the Literacy Program found her a church within twenty minutes walk from her home. She could take her children with her in a double stroller she received at the PRC. After several years in the program, she found a job, bought a secondhand car, and got a driver's license.

Space for tutoring was very limited for the Literacy Program until the Megan Bradshaw Learning Center was opened in 2005 in the newly acquired Naperville Road building. Prior to that opening, the Literacy Program had to share space with the Women's Wisdom Program. The Megan Bradshaw Center included an open tutoring area, a language lab, office space, and a playroom for child care. The Center allowed for a substantial expansion of literacy activities and more contact by clients with other PRC programs.

Still another aspect of the Literacy Program took shape in 2006. Working with DuPage United, an interfaith initiative, the PRC partnered with Faith Lutheran Church in Glen Ellyn and the Muslim Mohammed Webb Foundation to offer interfaith ESL classes. In order for Muslim community members to meet with members of other religious faiths, they felt a need for more fluency in English. The twofold goal of learning better English and meeting with members of other religious communities was expressed in a newspaper article on August 17, 2006, in the *Glen Ellyn News/Wheaton Leader.* Writing of Muslims, the article notes, "There is a real feeling of isolation in the community." Weekly meetings began to take place in September of 2006 in Faith Lutheran Church. Its Glen Ellyn location was ideal because World Relief settled many refugees in an apartment complex across the street from the church. Volunteer babysitters at the church and the volunteer tutors acted as cultural mentors for the newcomer families, helping them get to appointments and preparing tax returns.

Another link with a local Muslim community was the initiative taken by Maimoona Khan of the Villa Park Islamic Foundation. She had the idea of starting a Women's Conversation Group in a neighborhood where many women who could not drive were living. By helping women improve their English-language skills, this partnership has enabled women to pass driver's license tests, enroll in community college classes, and gain U.S. citizenship. Through this contact, the local Muslim community has invited staff and volunteers to their mosque and has hosted events at the PRC to discuss Islam.

Events centered on cultural understanding such as discussions of Islam and Spanish-language classes for staff and volunteers, have emphasized a realization that developed early in the Literacy

Wall in Literacy Program's
Megan Bradshaw Learning Center

Program's growth: "Every person is a learner." Interaction between students and tutors was recognized as a two-way street. The book club the PRC started, for instance, had both literacy students and PRC personnel as participants. The club's selections have aimed to acquaint all at the Center with the great variety and richness of world cultures, some of which the Literacy Program students themselves represented.

Maryanna Milton was hired in 2003 and became director of the Literacy Program seven years later. In 2004, the program had 96 volunteers and about 300 students. In 2010, the number of students had almost doubled to 597 and they were being taught by 160 volunteers. In 2011, a second classroom and language lab were started at the PRC facility in Westmont. The program received between ten and twenty inquiries a week and has had a waiting list as high as one hundred people wanting to study. The Program's offerings have been divided into two categories:

1. One-on-one or small group sessions: Trained volunteers help students with ESL, basic reading and writing, math skills, GED preparation, and citizenship test preparations in twenty-one locations.

2. ESL classes, Adult Basic Education (ABE), and General Education Development (GED).

a. College of DuPage conducts ESL courses at PRC locations in Wheaton and Westmont.

b. Head Start Parent ESL classes offered in partnership with CDI (formerly LifeLink) Head Start in Wheaton and Addison. Transportation and child care are provided from Head Start resources.

c. Women's conversation class in partnership with an Islamic Foundation offers small multilevel ESL classes.

d. GED/ABE classes, one-on-one or in small groups in Wheaton.

e. GED in Spanish in partnership with the Sisters of St. Joseph of LaGrange, Illinois.

f. Saturday chats: Advanced English conversation at the PRC.

g. Book club: Members choose books that describe the situation in a particular country or a region of the immigrants' homelands.

h. Training of volunteer tutors and instructors at the PRC.

This list is an impressive factual description of the Literacy Program's work, but the true spirit of volunteers and students working together has been best described in the story of one of its students, Rosa. In 2001, Rosa first came in contact with the PRC through an ESL class for Head Start parents. Because of her obvious motivation, Rosa was introduced to a volunteer tutor when the ESL class ended. She and the tutor met for more than two years, working first on basic English skills and then more specifically on the vocabulary she needed to pursue her goal of getting a cosmetology license. As their Friday morning meetings continued, Rosa's tutor became a mentor, advocate, and friend. Rosa passed her licensing exam in 2004 and began working as a hairdresser. Unable to open her own salon, she trained as an aerobics instructor and added a part-time job in that field. Still in contact with her tutor, Rosa accepted the tutor's suggestion to become the PRC's Spanish-as-Second-Language instructor. She taught volunteers, staff, and clients, and then, in 2006, she realized her dream to open a salon and day spa. Rosa's success story, though extraordinary, is not unique. The Literacy Program has been the gateway through which many clients have found a road to accomplishing their dreams. Like many of the PRC's programs past and present, Literacy depended on the leadership of women for its success. Pam Knight and Maryanna Milton have had a vision of what could be done by dedicated and skillful volunteers. The partnerships they have established have had a profound effect on a large number of DuPage County residents. The learning community formed at the PRC extended far beyond the number of those who took classes or were tutored. Families have had their prospects improved and groups have come together to establish greater understanding of each other. Pam, who has been a volunteer since the 1980s and on staff since 1999, is responsible for connecting adult client/students with needed educational services, classes, and tutorials for ESL, GED, ABE, and citizenship. She has also worked with volunteer tutors and with partner organizations to make education accessible. Over the years, she developed a succinct view of what the Literacy Program does:

"We are planting seeds of peace."

Computer Services

Paul Lefort introduced a few volunteers to the use of computers in the early 1980s, but it wasn't until 1992 that computerization of the PRC itself began. It was then that Dorothy from the PRC and Rosie Dixon representing Latinos Unidos, along with representatives from Hope, the DuPage Emergency Shelter, and Mary Ellen Durbin, then with Catholic Charities, joined to write an application to Apple Computers to create a countywide digital network. A group went to California for training and all received Apple Three-E computers for their organizations. Dorothy's idea was to link as many social service agencies as possible in DuPage County via a computer network. The services at this point were only to help the administration establish databases for donors and to facilitate client intake.

In 1993 Bob Dwyer approached Dorothy and suggested the establishment of a computer instruction program at the PRC. Bob and his wife, Mary Jean, were among the original members of the Religious Education Community and thus knew Dorothy well. Bob, an architect, knew the value of computers and saw their possibilities for handicapped persons who were among the PRC's clients. When the Center moved to its Roosevelt Road location, Bob took on the task of supervising the remodeling that was necessary for the building. He designed the handicapped access for the building with the idea that those in wheelchairs would be easily able to attend computer classes. Bob was not able to carry out his plan because of a fatal illness, but two years later another REC member stepped up to bring the idea to fruition. In 1995, Frank Goetz retired from his job as an engineer at Bell Labs, later Lucent Technology (now called Alcatel-Lucent), and offered his expertise in computers to Mary Ellen Durbin, the incoming executive director.

Frank's goal for computer services was twofold: first, to computerize the administration of the PRC and related agencies, DuPage PADS, and the medical and dental clinics. And second, to bridge the digital divide by offering computer training programs directly to clients.

Frank became a full-time volunteer and computerized the PRC'S administrative systems, especially the intake forms. The theft, in early 1995, of the few computers at the PRC meant a new database had to be developed almost from scratch. In addition, technical knowledge and support at the PRC and the other agencies were minimal at that time. Most of the technical talent acquired over the years for the PRC's own IT Department was drawn from the computer program volunteers who worked with Frank: John Victor, Roger Libman, Dave Gibson, and Ted Lind.

As these volunteers computerized the organization they developed the computer instruction and repair program. Mary Ellen was heavily involved in getting the Literacy Program started, and so it was not until spring 1996 that she was free enough to take steps to initiate a computer program. Knowing about a group in Detroit called Focus Hope, Mary Ellen suggested to Frank and others that they find out what Focus Hope was doing. Nine people made the trip and found out that the Detroit group had similarities to the early PRC. Eleanor Josuitis and Father Bill Cunningham had worked together to provide help for the many Detroit high school graduates who were deficient in reading and writing. Focus Hope raised the competency of these graduates and then provided machinist training for a year. Josuitis, like Dorothy, had a large family and was running a large food pantry with Cunningham's help. Focus Hope had branched out to train clients as machinists, opening new avenues for job searches.

Using a PowerPoint presentation, Frank began contacting friends and community leaders to explore the transfer possibilities of the Detroit model. Just as the founders of the Art Program had gone to California to bring back the idea of Women's Wisdom, so Frank came back from his trip to Michigan convinced that a training program could be established on what he had learned from Focus Hope. His expertise was computers and he knew computer literacy would be a help for clients.

A year after the trip to Detroit, Frank was contacting former colleagues from Lucent to see what kind of support he could round up to begin a computer program that would give clients help in getting jobs in the digital age. An unlikely source, Sister Lynn Shafer, contacted him from the Franciscan residential complex called Marian Park. She told Frank that a benefactor had donated three PCs that were fully operational with Windows and Microsoft Word software. Frank agreed to teach residents if they showed interest and Sister Lynn distributed flyers advertising the opportunity. Twelve people responded and Frank organized them into four classes that met one day a week for a year. Frank learned while teaching because his experience had not been with the Windows operating system. He had an immediate success because one of his students, Debbie Suggs, was able to get a job as an administrative assistant and database administrator. She later returned as a volunteer instructor after the program had been established. The computers for these early classes came from individuals, businesses such as Marianjoy Rehab Center, Waste Management, and the Federal Reserve Bank, and hospitals, principally from Central DuPage Hospital.

While he taught his class, Frank was spreading the word about his idea of a full-scale program at the PRC. Some of those who heard about this program began dropping off used electronic equipment on the covered back porch of the Roosevelt Road building. The equipment got in the way of food distribution, so Frank persuaded Mary Ellen to lease a nearby storefront that came to be called the Enrichment Center. The rear half of this new space was used for storing, testing, and refurbishing donated computers, monitors, and printers. Most of the work was done on Friday evenings by techies from Lucent and other local industries. Frank supplied the pizza and challenged participants to get enough equipment into working condition so that interested clients would have access to computers as they learned how to use them.

Word about the computer program continued to spread and Frank was able to deliver refurbished computers to a Naperville church so that a volunteer there could start classes in computer literacy. It was 1998 and the fledgling program already had a second training site. Since the Enrichment Center was serving as a home to four other programs, the need for more computer training and refurbishing sites quickly became apparent. The PRC's board of directors also used the Enrichment Center for its meetings and board members became aware of the need for more computer sites as they viewed the stacks of computers and monitors in the rear of the old store. They approved more rented space in Wheaton and were kept informed of the rapid expansion that was taking place.

Frank Goetz, founder of the Computer Program, at the opening
of the Enrichment Center. This narrow storefront housed the
computers in need of refurbishing, the Women's Wisdom Art
Program and ESL classes. It was also used for board meetings.

One of those expansions was in Woodridge where the police department operated a food and clothing distribution center. Frank
and his growing volunteer staff supplied the department with computers and began recruiting volunteers to do the instructing. Ted
Lind was one of those recruited. He supervised the creation and
continuous evolution of the computer curriculum for about a decade. He also supervised the volunteer computer instructors and
quality control through a well-constructed testing and student
feedback system, while continuing to teach classes.

Volunteers were essential to the growing program, but they needed someone more continually involved. The PRC hired Jeff Yamada who was a skilled computer technician and Hope Presbyterian Church in Wheaton provided Jeff a room for storage and refurbishing. Frank continued to supply the pizza as Jeff brought in more volunteers. With the increased supply of used equipment came a problem that threatened the whole operation, electronic waste. Not all the donated equipment could be made usable and that meant there had to be a place where the waste could be disposed of safely and legally. Frank's chance meeting with Linda Post was another of those miracles that the PRC routinely relied upon. Linda's husband owned United Recycling Industries in West Chicago and had as a company policy to provide public service. At no cost, United Recycling provided environmentally sound and legal disposal of computers and other equipment that could not be used. Frank transported the waste to the United Recycling plant in his own car until another volunteer took over that task.

By the year 2000, the growing Computer Program had hired a second employee, Rosalie Higgins, as an administrative assistant to register the growing number of people who wanted to take classes and to coordinate the distribution of refurbished computers to those who finished their courses. Rosalie's work gave Frank more free time to look around DuPage County and the rest of the country for those who were engaged in similar activities. Working with the College of DuPage, he was able to organize a meeting that he called "Bridging the Digital Divide Summit." He and Don Samuelson, a lawyer and former Peace Corps member, were not able to attract the political and industrial leaders they invited, but they did get the attention of social service organizations. The PRC's activity in the area of computer literacy was becoming more widely known.

The board of directors was also taking notice of the Computer Program's growth. Using another rented storefront on Gables Street in Wheaton, Frank had advertised the operation as People's Computer Resource Center, PCRC. This was a red flag because the board felt that the initials, "PRC," were too well known to make modifications that might confuse both clients and donors. But an even larger issue came before the board, the legality of what Frank was doing. Software that came with contributed computers was li-

Window display at the
Gables Computer Center

censed to the original
owner. Simply donating
the machine did not auto-
matically transfer that
license. For three years,
Frank's techies had been
installing operating sys-
tems other than Microsoft
Windows into refurbished
computers, but Windows
was the standard for PCs
and clients taking courses needed to learn how to use it.

Frank quickly learned that Microsoft was not about to allow free
licensing for refurbished computers. He decided to seek political
help for solving the problem. Henry Hyde was the Congressman in
the district and Keith Suchy, president of the board, was able to
arrange a meeting with Hyde. The allotted fifteen minutes was
extended to forty-five as Hyde became interested and called in
his staff members to formulate a plan. The Congressman, however, envisioned an attack on Microsoft's monopolistic practices
through the House Judiciary Committee. He conditioned any
Committee help on Frank's ability to come up with a legal brief
that the Committee's lawyers could use. Frank thought that local
law professors and their students would jump at the chance to prepare such a brief. Such interest, he found, was not there and so he
had to try another approach.

At this point, Frank came before the board and presented his
problem. What he was already doing was extensive in scope with
training sites functioning in ten suburbs and an ongoing refurbishing site preparing computers for successful trainees. The board
recognized that the Computer Program was a solid component of
the PRC, but the licensing problem made it a potential hazard.
Frank explained his dilemma in detail and received an immediate
and unanimous response: the board could not sanction anything
that was illegal or gave any appearance of illegality. Frank then
told the board members that he had two alternatives. The first was
to continue converting to open source (free) software—Linux and
Star Office—in place of Microsoft Windows and Word. This alternative was not ideal, but it was legal.

The second, and more ambitious alternative, entailed going through an intermediary to Bill Gates. Microsoft's founder was not easily accessible, but Frank found out that Rev. Jesse Jackson of Operation Push was going to meet with Gates in Palo Alto, California. A member of the PRC board, Rev. Andre Allen, was involved in a workshop at Operation Push and was able to arrange a meeting with Rev. Jackson. The meeting was short but Rev. Jackson finally asked Frank what he wanted. Frank's answer was, "Talk to Bill Gates." Jackson countered with, "I'll do better, I'll write him a letter." Frank wrote a draft of a letter and Rev. Jackson's staff prepared it and had him sign it. Rev. Jackson handed the letter to Bill Gates at the Palo Alto meeting and Frank began calling Microsoft to find out what the company would do.

The letter progressed through Microsoft's company channels slowly. The best answer Frank could get was, "They're working on it." Finally, however, the answer came through that Microsoft had instituted a new program, "Microsoft Authorized Refurbisher" (MAR). The PRC became the first nonprofit to take part in the program because all refurbished computers were given to clients free. The PRC absorbed the nominal cost of getting a new license for each computer.

In 2003, John Victor joined the computer program and his expertise made him a perfect fit for the new job of technology director. The PRC was preparing to move into its newly acquired building on Naperville Road in Wheaton. Frank wanted the program to be visible to all clients and was able to get a room set aside as a training site on the main floor of the new building directly across from the reception desk. Michael Birck, the president of Tellabs, provided a substantial start-up grant to equip the room with desks and computers and a large window through which those working could easily be seen. Once the new building opened, this room housed the Tellabs Computer Literacy Training and Access Program (CLTA). Clients entering could not help but see the facility and all were told that they were eligible to join the classes. It was from those who applied for computer training that Luciano Rodriguez assembled the class that combined both English and computer literacy at St. Paul's Lutheran Church in Wheaton. When the PRC moved into its newly renovated building, computer training, with John as director, went into operation there along with the repair and refurbishing unit on the second floor. The building's basement began to fill up with donated computers and by the end of the year, the program was able to report its progress to that point in the PRC's 2004/2005 annual report.

Computer training and access in fifteen DuPage County locations:

— 885 students in computer classes
— 1,947 families received refurbished computers
— 2,783 visits were made to the Computer Training Center
— 437 computer repairs made

Before Frank retired from the Computer Program, he had two volunteers who would become the mainstays of refurbishing and repair activities, John Victor and Roger Libman. Roger had joined the program in 2002 and would remain to become a full-time volunteer. He and John had worked out of the Computer Center when it was located on Gables Street, but the Program was also using many other sites scattered around the county. Both did refurbishing of donated computers that were to be given to clients who successfully finished the courses. By 2004, they, and the volunteers who worked with them, had refurbished or repaired more than a thousand computers. They found that some clients already had computers so they expanded their operation to include repairs on all machines regardless of their origin. This service was open to clients, volunteers, and staff, but was limited to one computer per family per year.

Volunteer Roger Libman
refurbishing a donated computer

In 2005, with the move to the larger building on Naperville Road, the Computer Program had the luxury of a repair room and a classroom setting for computer literacy training. John and Roger set up a larger refurbishing and repair facility. They concentrated on this aspect of the program, making it a separate operation that attracted tech-minded volunteers at the rate of twenty-five to thirty a year. These volunteers were retirees with computer backgrounds, high school students, and those who were looking for jobs and wanted work with the PRC on their résumés. Hired originally as director of computer services, John was able to extend repair work to include other non-profits with historical ties to the PRC, DuPage PADS, and the DuPage Community Clinic. John also found himself being asked for references as some of his volunteers were able to get paying jobs because of their experience at the PRC. Roger found a special niche. He combined his computer expertise with a flair for communications to become the unofficial recorder of the PRC's growth. He put together DVDs for occasions like open house receptions and celebrations for staff retirements. Taken together, his electronic pictorial collections are an ongoing record of growth. The saying at the PRC is "If you want anything on video, ask Roger." Graphics for these presentations were done by Dave Gibson. Both of them put in many volunteer hours to produce the videos.

Describing the work of volunteers and staff in the Computer Program does not provide the full picture of what has been accomplished. On a tapestry, created by Martha Tavis, that hangs outside the door of the computer refurbishing room on the second floor in Wheaton, there are short testimonials taken from letters that the PRC received from those who benefited from the classes they had taken. The writers are a cross-section of the PRC's clientele.

> I am very glad about this program because we are refugees. I have been in United States for eight months. I could not find a proper job because I am disable[d] and in Sudan I was lawyer so I need to find some skills like computers. To all my thanks, *Mohamed*.

> I am seventy years old and lost my husband and two adult children in the last eight years. I have no one here in Illinois. I started my first computer class and love it. I have a great teacher. If it weren't for the People's Resource Center I would not know anything about computers. With the printer I can make cards for my grandchildren. Thanks, *Delores*

> The PRC is the place to turn for answers for employment and retraining issues. This organization was a great blessing to my family at a time when we lost our home and had not yet

been able to obtain other help. Without reliance on miracles, my family would be in worse circumstances than we are. Thanks again for your time and insight. Sincerely, *Myriam*

I have a six-year-old daughter who is mentally retarded. She will use the computer for phonics and special learning needs. I also have a nine-year-old daughter in third grade who will use the computer for maps and reports. I am going back to school for medical billing and decoding to work from home so I can spend more time with my children, thank you, *Theresa*

I have been attending classes in Addison to enable me to re-search my disease on the internet. My last chemo damaged my heart so I can no longer get chemo. I want to research similar cases and show successful options when I attend roundtable sessions with my doctors. Respectfully submit-ted, *Judith*

I am using my computer to awaken my mind, spirit, and soul. It has given me self-esteem and a chance to be equal with ev-eryone else. You can't see my wheelchair nor my severe arthritic fingers and body. With the help of my patient in-structors I'm on my way. I would like a printer to remind myself of my accomplishments. Thanks for your generous and hard work, *Minnie*

I would like to request a printer for my daughter who is a high school senior. As a mother, my heart is breaking, no peace of mind, always worried when she walks home late from the li-brary or a friend's to use the computer for homework. Now I have peace of mind. My family is thankful for the PRC who have the heart to help an indigent family. God bless, *Carina*

The tapestry on which these testimonials are displayed is a con-stant reminder to everyone that life can be made a little better for clients through the work of volunteers and staff. It is not just the computer that helps solve problems, it is the feeling, imparted by teachers and refurbishers, that each person who participated in the program became a part of the PRC's caring community. The mes-sages on the tapestry also show that computers are for more than getting jobs. They make life easier for the disabled and a bit safer for teenagers.

From 1993 to 2012, more than 10,000 donated and refurbished computers were distributed, but there was still much to be done in order to provide computer access to many more people. According to the winter 2012 edition of *Digital Domain,* a PRC in-house publication, 40 percent of low-income households had not yet entered the digital age. As early as 1999, the PRC's newsletter, called *Life Lines,* carried the following quote that summed up the importance of the enrichment and empowerment programs: "The Computer Program, along with Women's Wisdom and the Literacy Program, are the current vehicles with which we hope to provide access to mainstream society. The Center is committed to give people opportunities to escape poverty."

Jobs Assistance Program

In 2005, a group of volunteers began to meet because they perceived a need and decided to address it. The Computer Training Program gave clients technical skills, but those skills did not automatically guarantee job placement. Other skills and information were necessary before computer "graduates" could enter the labor force and make a living.

Frank had retired from the computer program and Barbara Tartaglione had just come to the PRC as a volunteer whose experience was as a professional career counselor in workforce development. John Slusarski was already working at the PRC, helping Hurricane Katrina victims find jobs in the Chicago area. Mary Blair was also active in computer training and Julie Varvaro was a new volunteer with a degree in education. Together they formed a steering committee and spent a year planning and launching the Jobs Assistance Program.

Their first task was to find mentors for job seekers. They succeeded in finding sixteen qualified people. Mentoring was a basic necessity because PRC clients needed more than just an employment agency. Those clients who sought the program's services often faced multiple barriers to employment. The counselors had first to assess the needs and abilities of the job-seeking client. This could prove to be a lengthy process. Résumé development was also often difficult because many of the clients had weak employment histories. In addition, most clients needed help exploring the range of job and career opportunities open to them and all required aid in getting ready for interviews.

Dennis McCann succeeded Frank as director of Computer Training in 2005 and then assumed the directorship of Job Assistance as that program developed. Two years later, John Slusarski made contact with the Chicago Jobs Council and formed a relationship with the PRC's program that led to the formation of the West Suburban Jobs Council. This group brought together all the agencies that did employment counseling in DuPage County and provided professional development for job coaches. It also initiated advocacy for job seekers with multiple barriers to employment, immigrants, those with disabilities, the homeless, and victims of domestic violence.

The PRC's Jobs Assistance program began with mentoring clients on a one-to-one basis and organizing workshops in which the job seekers could interact with each other as well as with mentors. An important element was added to the program in 2011 when Debbie Lunger was hired to develop contacts with potential employers. By that year, the program, which had extended to the PRC in Westmont, was serving more than 200 job seekers per month.

The merger of the Computer Training and Jobs Assistance programs has proved to be an important empowerment step for clients. In 2011, almost 1,900 students were enrolled in Computer Training classes. Most of them would become job seekers as they finished the classes. They would not have far to go for help. In summary, the four empowerment programs that enabled clients to obtain self-help skills added a new dimension to the activities of the Center that had, up to this point, addressed only basic needs.

7

Financial and Human Resources

Getting the Job Done

W HEN REC first began to meet at Maryknoll College in the late 1960s, there was little need for fund-raising. The Center paid no rent at the College and there was no paid staff. The only expense was printing and postage for the *REC Bulletin*. The labor to produce the *Bulletin* was volunteer. It was not until 1976 that formal accounts were kept. Between 1976 and 1990 Margaret Roth managed one combined account for REC and the PRC. The account book for that period recorded checks for bills paid or contributions made by REC/PRC. Money contributed to either entity was listed simply as donations without any reference to its source. For the first four years of this record keeping, total contributions ranged from $1,000 to $2,100 per year.

By August 1980, the PRC was incorporated and had obtained its own tax-exemption number, but all checks were still written on an account shared with REC. Contributions increased so that by 1984, income was $35,838. Some of that amount came from REC members, but no separate record was kept for them. REC did not start its own separate checking account until 1990.

In the twenty years from 1990 to 2010, Margaret, assisted at various times by Eileen LeFort, Bobbie Perkins, and Fran Holtzman, collected more than $83,000 in the REC account. About 85 percent of that amount went to the PRC. REC support was then and continues to be rent paid for the room used on Sunday mornings, monthly contributions to Family Connections, and yearly support of the PRC's Thanksgiving dinner program and "Share the Spirit" at Christmas time. REC also always purchased at least one table at the PRC's Galas.

The interconnection between REC and the PRC was, however, more than just monetary. From its inception, the PRC's board of directors has been a voluntary service and at least one, and as many as three, REC members served on that board at any given time. The Food Pantry and the Clothes Closet were begun with REC volunteers and as these programs grew, REC members continued to serve in these programs and in all the PRC's later programs.

Dorothy McIntyre was a REC member, of course, one of the earliest. Her work, from the PRC's beginning until her death in 1994, was all without compensation. In fact, those close to the PRC's early days were convinced that Dorothy was using some of her own money to pay at least part of the expenses of the organization.

Two themes, like two sides of a coin, recur continually in the history of the PRC: constant increase in the needs of clients and the crescendo of calls for donors to meet those needs. The ongoing miracle that Dorothy relied upon was that unfailing response whenever the needs became critical. Mary Ellen Durbin later expressed the same sentiment in a more spiritual way: "I know there are angels in this world. We always seem to get help when we need it the most." And Carol McHaley, brought the theme back to earth: "We live like some of the families we serve—from week to week."

Some of the miracles have already been mentioned in this history, but there are others. One of the many times that the food pantry was running short on canned goods and staples, a Girl Scout troop came through the door with boxes of canned food they had collected in a food drive. Then, there was a staff meeting called to address and brainstorm a specific need, back-to-school items for school-aged children of clients. Literally, thirty minutes after the meeting ended a man called and wanted to make a generous and anonymous donation, but he wanted it to go for a present need. When he learned about the school supplies concerns, he sent a check to cover the school supplies and he has been a regular donor every year since.

The PRC was founded to provide for human needs, but, at times, it has also been in need. The following headlines and quotes that have appeared in various publications capture those needs:

Chicago Tribune, August 12, 1991: "Clinic, Food Pantry Caught in a Bind. [PRC] Could Lose Their Rental House in Wheaton." Carol McHaley is quoted in the article: "I wonder every day now where the next dollar is coming from and whether we'll have a roof over our heads tomorrow."

Daily Herald, September 11, 1992: "Pantries Hurting in Wake of Disasters." The PRC is receiving less because people are giving money to the victims of Hurricane Andrew and to civil war victims in Yugoslavia.

Chicago Tribune, August 9, 1994: "Area Pantries Report Cupboards Are Bare." Dorothy McIntyre, executive director of People's Resource Center in Wheaton, which supplies food to about 150 families a week, says that she expects to run out of food this week.... "We turn people away every week, this is just a problem out here that isn't going away. About 45 percent of the people we see are working poor." McIntyre said when People's Resource Center opened fourteen years ago, it was envisioned as a temporary emergency agency, but through the years, it has evolved into a vital community resource. "We used to see people get up on their feet. Now its chronic," McIntyre said.

Chicago Tribune, 1994: "Charities Struggle to Meet High Demand for Help." The line outside the nonprofit PRC pantry isn't a blip on any economic radar screen, according to officials of public and private agencies who serve DuPage's poor.... While nobody is declaring a crisis yet, the steadily increasing and unusual repeat demands for interim assistance for food, shelter, rent, utility bills, and medical care are showing signs of straining the human safety net that belies DuPage's affluent image.

Daily Herald, October 27, 1995: "Demand High at People's Resource Center." Quoting Al White, "I haven't seen it like this in ten years of volunteering. One Tuesday morning this month, we had 180 families lined up for food."

Flood damage at the PRC was also reported in a number of publications:

The Catholic Explorer, November 14, 1997: "Sewer Backup
Causes Damage at People's Resource Center." Within three
days of a recent sewer backup that caused $11,000 to $20,000
damage to the food pantry at PRC, more than $11,000 worth
of donations from private and corporate sources poured in to
ease the burden on the social service agency.… All food and
lots of clothing was lost.… Despite immediate financial set-
backs, individuals and corporations have remedied the
situation with bountiful donations. Mary Ellen Durbin is
quoted: "By Tuesday, the most amazing thing began to happen. We have recouped almost all of the lost food. People
came in with $5 and $10 bills. Loaves and Fishes in Naperville called and said, 'We have such an abundance right now
of cereal and pasta and spaghetti.' The hair stood up on my
hands because that's exactly what we needed."

The Wheaton Leader, November 2, 1997: "Halloween Sewer
Backup Scary for Resource Center." The Wheaton Kiwanis
donated more than $100 and will build shelves in the base-
ment to prevent a repeat accident. Bethlehem Center also
chipped in.

Daily Herald, November 15, 1997: "Wheaton Residents
Quick To Rescue." Within a few days after the sewer backup,
civic groups, businesses, and individuals donated about
$12,000 and money is still coming in.

Chicago Tribune, November 4, 1997: "After Flood, Food
Pantry in Wheaton Stays Afloat." Eight thousand pounds of
food had to be thrown away, but rather than shutting down,
PRC used some of its cash reserves to purchase eggs and
bread and $25 grocery food certificates for 200 families.

The headlines above could not have been written if the PRC did
not have friends who were ready to step up when needs were most
pressing. One story that did not make the headlines was told by
Mary Ellen after her retirement in 2010:

When I came to the PRC in 1995, the organization had recently experienced a robbery, in which all the computers and

telephones were stolen. One of the first administrative decisions was to install a security system at the PRC. Along with
the loss of the computers was the loss of a donor database.
Together with some of the volunteers, I pieced together a list
of PRC supporters and we were able to publish an annual report in July 1995. Within a few months, it became clear that
the PRC, although it enjoyed a solid reputation among non-
profits in DuPage, and had a dedicated core of volunteers,
was struggling for survival as an organization due to lack of
funds. We were facing a severe budget deficit. The board recommended writing a letter to our known supporters to ask for
their help. That letter generated almost $20,000. That
amount, coupled with a very generous contribution from the
Wheaton Franciscan System, Inc., saved the organization for
that fiscal year. It was the combined effort of individuals,
foundations, corporations, schools, churches, social service
organizations, and government that has made the PRC's
work possible.

Individual Donations

The People's Resource Center was never a governmental or church-
affiliated agency. From its inception, it was a small group, providing help to those in need; its funding came from individual
contributors who believed in its mission. The support consisted of
monetary and in-kind donations as well as large numbers of volunteer work hours. Two early PRC supporters had the backing of
their respective Benedictine religious communities. Sister Benita
of the Benedictine Sisters of the Sacred Heart Monastery and
Brother Finian of the Benedictine Fathers of St. Procopius Abbey
were both affiliated with Illinois Benedictine College (now, Benedictine University) in Lisle. The support of these two religious
communities was on an ad hoc basis and never involved any effort
to influence or control the fledgling organization.

References already made to individual donations speak to both
the motivations of these supporters and the kinds of contributions
they made. In-kind donations began as canned food when REC
met on Sunday mornings. As REC members spread the word,
clothing began to come in to the Clothes Closet from many sources
and then computers from both individuals and institutions. Over

the years, the early letters that Dorothy sent to a few friends have evolved into an extensive combination of appeals through regular mass mailings, a newsletter, and events that reach a far wider group of supporters from all over DuPage County and well beyond its borders. All of these efforts are still aimed at individuals because they represent the basic resource for the People's Resource Center.

In 2011 individual donations represented 34 percent of the Center's total revenue. Depending on the state of the U.S. economy, these donations have fluctuated between 20 and 40 percent of total funding received during the most recent decade. Major gifts from individuals have consistently been the largest portion of these funds. The largest actual number of donations, however, has come from the many contributors who regularly send checks and sometimes drop in personally to leave cash at the Wheaton and Westmont locations. The trend, even allowing for peaks and valleys in the national economy, has been a slow but steady increase in monetary contributions. This has been the unpublicized "miracle" because it is a steady cash flow and has so often been overshadowed by the large gifts that arrived just when the needs of the organization were critical. Likewise, in-kind donations have followed the same upward slant. Though there is no statistical record of other in-kind gifts, the computer program illustrates this upward trend. In the fiscal year 2001–2002, the program distributed 550 refurbished computers to clients who had successfully finished the training course. Ten years later, that number is 1,000, and all computers distributed are in-kind donations. On the other hand, Rent/Mortgage Assistance, a federal program administered by the PRC, has remained constant with between 220 and 250 families served over the last decade. This is due in part to the fact that government funds have remained the same or in some years have been reduced.

One particular donation stands out as legendary at the PRC. Just before Thanksgiving each year, volunteers distribute turkeys to clients. One year, after the last turkey had been given out, twelve people were still waiting in the living room of the house on Indiana Avenue. The volunteers were just about to tell those clients that there were no turkeys left, when a van pulled up outside and its driver came to the door. He greeted the volunteer who met him at the door with the words, "I've got a dozen turkeys in the van, can you use them?" The turkeys were quickly given out, and the PRC witnessed another of its miracles.

Donations by Organizations

The individual donor base, however, does not diminish the importance of organizations that have also been a mainstay of the PRC's efforts. These organizations represent a significant cross section of the variety of groups found in DuPage County.

Religious Organizations

The first institutional grants the PRC received came from the Catholic Diocese of Joliet. Over time both Catholic and Protestant churches, especially those in Wheaton and Glen Ellyn, have contributed substantial financial resources as well as providing space and volunteers and holding food drives. Churches have also provided space for PRC functions. "Share the Spirit" Christmas distributions began in a church and the early Computer Program found storage space and classrooms in churches. The Literacy Program would not be as extensive as it is today without churches that provide facilities for students and teachers to meet. The early presence of the PRC in Westmont was in the basement of the Alliance Church. Without churches and other religious groups, the work of serving clients would have been very limited as the number of those clients increased steadily. The Franciscan Sisters of Wheaton have played an important role in providing significant monetary contributions at times when the PRC was running short of funds, and they have contributed many uncounted volunteer hours as board members for many years.

Schools

From kindergarten through university, schools have given the PRC a great deal of support. High school students have been especially active in the Christmas program, collecting gifts and volunteering for the display and distribution of gifts. Both middle and high school students have organized food drives. Wheaton College has sent both volunteers and interns, and Benedictine University has taken an initiative in supporting the early medical program and more recently the housing program. Many DuPage school districts have donated their older computers for refurbishing and redistribution.

Associations

Members of a wide variety of associations have assisted through fund-raising, in-kind donations, and volunteering. These associations include Boy and Girl Scout troops, fraternal and service organizations, clubs, guilds, and retirement communities. Volunteers from many organizations have cleaned up after floods, built shelving for food, and painted offices and meeting rooms. In 1998, Cub Scout Pack 89 organized a "Bucket Brigade." They filled ninety-two buckets with cleaning supplies and equipment and distributed them to clients. The Glen Ellyn Rotary Club contributed a substantial amount to help buy new computers after the 1995 burglary.

Businesses

Companies, banks, hospitals, large retail stores, and the U.S. Post Office have all contributed to the growth of the PRC with funds and volunteers who come on company time. In-kind donations from local businesses have run the gamut of products from stocking caps, bicycles, pretzels, and diapers to school supplies and computers. The yearly collection of food by the Post Office has filled pantry shelves when the cupboard was almost bare. A creative form of giving was initiated by two volunteers, Sue Okarma and Judy Bonelli, when a few restaurants in Wheaton joined "Dine Away Hunger." The restaurants contributed 10 percent of their gross receipts on a given day and the PRC advertised the event. The number of participating restaurants has grown over the years because of the continuing efforts of these two volunteers and "Dine Away Hunger" is now almost a monthly event throughout the county.

The law firm of Sidley Austin has been a valuable resource for the PRC because of the pro bono work its attorneys have offered. Whenever the PRC needed legal work the firm allowed one or more of its members to provide pro bono services. These services would have been a serious financial drain on the Center if the attorneys had billed at their standard rates. The firm was especially helpful in setting up a Limited Liability Corporation (LLC) so that the PRC and the DuPage Community Clinic could occupy and jointly maintain the same building on Roosevelt Road. This LLC became the first such entity in Illinois to gain a tax-exempt status. Sidley Austin attorneys continue to aid the PRC with legal consultation on contracts.

Every two years or so, the PRC holds a "Gala" for which many businesses donate items to be auctioned. The first Galas were underwritten by Pete Conway and the CNA Insurance Company where he worked. Over the years, a number of companies have provided funds as they matched employee contributions to the PRC. The first was Stone Container's match of a donation by REC member Art Bostwick in the 1970s. An important business contribution was the cooperation and help given to the PRC's volunteers by managers and staff in local retail outlets during the Christmas rush season. Sales personnel in Kohl's, T.J.Maxx, Walmart, Jewel, and Dominicks have regularly helped volunteers to make large purchases for "Share the Spirit" families.

DuPage Community Foundation grant presented by board member Betty Bradshaw (right) to Mary Ellen Durbin (left) and board president Lyn Conway, November 1998

Grants

Initially, Dorothy McIntyre sought donations solely from individuals, but within a few years she realized that larger amounts of funding were necessary for the growing clientele. In 1990, she hired a part-time grant writer because writing applications was taking up too much of her time. The next year, she applied to the City of Wheaton to buy the Christian Blind Mission Building on Roosevelt Road, but she had to wait until 1992 for the award. Also in 1991, the PRC received two grants, one from the DuPage Community Foundation for $5,000 and one from DuPage County for $15,000. Both of these grants were to facilitate the opening of the DuPage Community Clinic, which was then still part of the PRC. Fifteen years after the PRC's founding, grants were becoming an important element in its financial resources. One example is the RJN Foundation, which REC member Richard Nogaj established in 1995. This Foundation has been a steady contributor to the PRC's activities since its inception.

Innovations

A number of novel fund-raising ideas were tried in PRC's early days. Al White initiated a "Spare Change" program by collecting small change at the front door of a Sam's Club store. The Walmart Foundation matched what was collected. As volunteers did free gift wrapping during holidays at Barnes & Noble stores, they collected both money and food. Bob Dwyer introduced the "Art of Barter," which brokered goods and services donated by its members into a tax write-off and provided vouchers to access the pool of donated goods and services. Entertainment became a source of funding when a quartet of students from Glenbard South High School sang in the school and collected contributions from fellow students and teachers. On a more professional level, Gavin Coyle has donated his talent to give a concert each year with a percentage of the proceeds going to the PRC.

Giving food items for freebies was an innovation of the Coffee Cup Coffee House in 1996. Anyone who brought in a nonperishable food item received a complimentary cup of coffee. In the same year, the Rousseau Chiropractic Group in Wheaton gave a free examination and X-ray to anyone who brought in a bag of food items for the PRC. JCPenney made the PRC a recipient in its national Fight for Hunger. Customers at their Yorktown Center store were given a 25 percent discount if they brought in a food contribution. The PRC not only received $1,350 from JCPenney, but volunteers were able to distribute literature and speak to people as they entered the store.

These "early days" fund-raising efforts have grown and expanded to meet the needs of many more clients. The growing population of DuPage County and the economic conditions of the first decade of the twenty-first century have required both creative thinking and a lot of hard work. The PRC now has a development team and the board of directors has a standing committee dedicated to suggesting and evaluating ideas for bringing in the resources to be given to those who come to the Center in need.

People Resources

The "People's" part of the PRC's name represents the other pole of the Resources spectrum. It was for people that the PRC was founded and it has been because of people that it has grown into an important member of DuPage County's resource network.

Volunteers

For a long time after the Center's founding, volunteers were the only personnel serving clients, and volunteers continue to be indispensable in its ability to serve ever-increasing numbers of the county's residents. An informal survey in the 1990s found that 30 percent of volunteers had been or continued to be clients. The reasons they gave for volunteering included "wanting to give back," "realizing that there were others in greater need than themselves," and "liking the community atmosphere" they found at the PRC. At a meeting of the board of directors, one board member told of how he had come to the PRC as a child with his parents, who were clients. He liked the people he met so much that he wanted to be part of the community he remembered.

As with funding, volunteers increased as the needs of clients increased. In many cases, they were recruited by REC members as when Frank Goetz asked his former colleagues at Lucent to contribute their skills to the early Computer Program. Similarly, Margaret Roth, as treasurer, asked her colleague Jeff Madura, an accounting professor, to prepare tax returns in the PRC's early years. Some volunteers for the Literacy Program heard about the program through churches or from those who were already clients of that program. Especially in the 1990s, when refugees from Southeast Asia, Africa, and Eastern Europe swelled the ranks of clients, more volunteers from these areas as well as other recent immigrants asked how they could help those whose problems they knew firsthand.

During the first decade of the twenty-first century, the number of active volunteers increased from 450 to over 1,300 and their hours of work grew from 22,000 in 2001 to 91,000 ten years later. Many have been with the PRC for years and in some cases, decades. At present, a staff member, Lisa Doyle, gives orientations for new volunteers twice every month and coordinates their activities so as to allow the time they can contribute to be used most effectively. The sheer numbers of volunteers led Linda Cheatham, in 2008, to formalize their activities under the Human Resources Department. This formalization also included screening, selection, training, and support in whichever program the volunteers were working. The continuing miracle of the PRC volunteers was expressed early by Dorothy and has been echoed ever since, "None of them have to come, but we always seem to have enough."

Staff

Between 1975 and 1984, the People's Resource Center was run entirely by volunteers. Five women, including Dorothy, took care of providing information and counseling at the very beginning. There was help in the Food Pantry and the Clothes Closet from REC members and others, and the only record of these early workers is what can be found in the surviving bulletins and newsletters that Dorothy wrote. No one was keeping official records because such documentation was considered unnecessary extra work. All of the early volunteers knew each other and already had more work than they could handle.

As has been mentioned, the first person to be paid officially was Janice Cagel. She had come through the ranks, client–volunteer–staff, and it was because of her work with food collection and distribution that she was hired to coordinate that part of the operation. There were no formal programs, but she was considered to be in charge of the pantry. By 1989, Carol McHaley became first the de facto director of the Food Pantry and then in 1990 she was appointed officially by Dorothy. With that position, Carol began receiving a small salary. Her main job was to do the weekly shopping to replenish the groceries that had been distributed on the previous Tuesday. She recalled that when she finished shopping and recorded what she had spent, she would ask Dorothy if there was enough money to shop again next week. Dorothy assured her there would be and there always was. It was another of the on-going miracles.

Dorothy was known to be making payments to some of the volunteers whom she deemed in most need. As such, she was just extending the scope of the PRC's mission. The distinction between volunteers and paid staff was blurred by feelings she had for anyone she considered needy. The distinction was to become a problem, however, in 1995, when Linda Cheatham began to organize the accounts and found that checks Dorothy had written were recorded as salaries for which no federal tax or Social Security had ever been withheld. Since Dorothy had died a year earlier, there was no way to mount a defense of her payments; back taxes, Social Security, and penalties had to be paid. The matter was settled with the IRS and Linda set up an accounting system that took care of all payments that were due the federal government from the payroll.

In contrast to the rapid rise in numbers of volunteers, the number of paid employees rose slowly. The number of full-time and part-time staff was nineteen in 2001. Ten years later, it was thirty-two. Although the number of staff is still small, the job description of each is supplemented by an employee handbook to better coordinate job-related activities and provide greater employee security. One of the challenges encountered in staffing is the unpredictability of federal government funds for the PRC's Housing Program. Federal funds for rent and mortgage assistance include money for administration of the funds. Those hired for this administrative work must be let go when the amount of funding decreases. Even with the increase in paid staff and recurring periods of economic uncertainty, however, the PRC has been able, throughout its history to devote at least ninety-five cents of every dollar it receives to direct services for its clients.

Board of Directors

Not long after Dorothy launched the People's Resource Center, she recruited a few REC members to help with the increasing workload that the infant organization quickly developed. This small group was not yet officially incorporated and thus did not technically need a board of directors, but Dorothy recognized that she needed help. This first informal "board" was led by Dorothy's neighbor and REC member Mary Ann Bostwick. It had as its primary function to help with fund-raising, but those involved became extenders of Dorothy's vision. When it became obvious that fund-raising had to go beyond Dorothy's immediate circle of friends and REC members, she enlisted her "board" to help in getting the PRC incorporated.

> On the 11th of October 1981, the first official meeting of the People's Resource Center was held at 102 West Indiana, Wheaton, Illinois, at 1:00 p.m., pursuant to a written call and notice to the directors.

So began the minutes of this organizing meeting. The resolutions that followed included acceptance of By-Laws, adoption of a corporate seal, approval of the articles of incorporation, and the choice of the Bank of Wheaton as a depository of funds. The final resolution of these minutes provided the names of the people who were elected as directors: Constance Gardner, Paul LeFort, Rosalie Placet, Charlotte Sommer, and Brother Finian Taylor.

All those named as directors in the resolution were members of REC. They were voted in as "members" of the new corporation because all had been directly involved in the operation of the PRC from its inception. Their official recognition on this occasion was the first time anything like a formal list of people involved in the work of the Center was compiled.

The existing copies of board minutes for meetings during the early 1980s indicate that the board did the basic work of approving expenditures and signing off on grant proposals. Dorothy was still very much in charge of what happened at the PRC. The next important item appeared in minutes of late 1992. It announced the real estate closing for the newly acquired building on Roosevelt Road. Federal money had been received by the City of Wheaton and the closing would take place when the formalities had been attended to by lawyers for all parties. A task force of Lyn Conway, Dorothy McIntyre, and Mary Ann Bostwick was to plan an open house in January or February of 1993 to which county and city elected officials would be invited as well as all volunteers.

When Dorothy died in 1994, Lyn, the board's president, did the work of finding candidates for the position of executive director. Approval of Dorothy's successor came after the board had interviewed Mary Ellen in early 1995. The PRC then expanded and with each new program, the Dental Clinic, Computer Training and Refurbishing, Literacy, and Art, the board made the serious decisions on whether the organization's finances could afford these expansions. As budgets became larger and committees were established, the committees on Finance and Fund Development provided oversight and ideas for income and expenditures. The New Programs Committee scrutinized ideas and recommended innovations for potential expansion. Mary Ellen inaugurated day-long retreats so that the board could do extended strategizing and also get to know the staff better. She also brought in professional consultants to familiarize board members with the latest developments in not-for-profit organizational development.

In the early years of the twenty-first century, the need for more space became critical and the Roosevelt Road building was deemed no longer adequate. The board appointed a Building Committee that began a long search for a suitable building. At the same time, the board approved a capital campaign to pay for a larger and better physical facility, one that would be more easily adapted to the number and kinds of programs the PRC then housed. After extensive renovation of the newly purchased building, the board decided that enough funds were available to approve an extension of the PRC operation in Westmont from a church basement to a rented office/warehouse. Finally, when Mary Ellen decided to retire in 2010, the board appointed a Search Committee that advertised the position, received and screened well over a hundred applications, and presented board members with five applicants from whom the present executive director, Kim Perez, was chosen. The Search Committee provided a professional level of screening and narrowing the field of applicants that made the board's final choice a very difficult one because of the exceptional qualifications of each finalist.

Over the years, the board remained the same while becoming different. As was the case from the beginning, all board members were volunteers and all joined the board because they knew of the PRC's work and wanted to become part of it. The difference, in recent years, has been in the professional backgrounds these members have brought to the board. The PRC has been able to attract to its governing body men and women in banking, finance, corporate management, marketing, and human relations as well as those with not-for-profit experience. Keith Suchy, for example, provided the dental expertise and organizing experience to get the Dental Clinic started. He later became president of the board, while remaining a practicing dentist and an officer in the Chicago Dental Association.

In much the same way, Tom Okarma brought his experience of running a business to the board before he became its president. Most recently, Barbara Tartaglione was elected board president and brought experience as a professional counselor in workforce development. An ongoing example of board members' dedication has been the large number who have also volunteered in a particular program of the PRC either while active board members or after retiring from it.

For most of the members, their participation in governance is not just another job, it is a vocation, and during their tenure on the board they come to consider themselves part of the PRC community.

Clients

The most important resource has always been those people who come through the Center's door in need of help. Their presence was the reason the PRC was founded and why it continues to exist. For some, coming through that door is very difficult because they never imagined that they would be in need. Margaret recounted the story of one client she met while doing intake at the rented house on Indiana Avenue:

> I was sitting by the window and saw a rather expensive car park outside the house. The woman who got out was well dressed and I expected that she would be making a donation. When she came in, however, I found she needed help. She

told me that she lived in a nice house with her mother because her husband had walked out on her and could not be found. He had taken their savings and the house was in both their names. Without him, the woman could not legally sell the house. She had a job, but her income was just enough to pay the mortgage. She knew that if she defaulted on the mortgage she would lose the house. Consequently, she and her mother had to live on her mother's Social Security. She needed help because all she had in the refrigerator was a couple of eggs.

Following the example Dorothy set, volunteers and staff make a point of treating each person with respect and letting each know that she or he is a guest whom it is an honor to serve. The intake process that a new client goes through is not a means of reducing that person to a statistic, but rather a way of getting to know him or her and finding out what services can address their particular needs. The hope is that all the PRC's guests will come to feel like part of the community. Reactions from clients usually include surprise that the people they meet sincerely care about their needs.

The PRC's staff has expanded to include a full-time social worker whose job it is to help clients assess their own needs in the light of what is offered in the PRC's programs and what referrals can be made. Volunteers and staff have found that people who come for food often need clothing, better housing, and tutoring for getting a GED or a better mastery of English. Once basic needs are addressed, they find that they can also get help in a job search and can get a referral for medical or dental care. This process has caused many of those who came in as clients to return to the PRC as volunteers and staff members. The present staff has found that a number of those who "come through the door" in search of help will come back later to offer their services as volunteers. Returning to volunteer is the highest compliment and the sincerest thanks anyone can give.

A few examples of client stories illustrate how they have been helped. These accounts are summarized from the *PRC Volunteers Newsletter*:

When "Bob" first came to the PRC, he was unemployed and behind in his rent. Fearing he would become homeless, he enrolled in Family Connections. The PRC's social worker found that he was a veteran but did not know that he was eligible for housing assistance. With the social worker's help, Bob got VA assistance and was able to move closer to his family and get their support.

"Miranda" gave birth shortly after being laid off from her job. The cost of diapers and formula were too much for Miranda and her husband. They came to the PRC and were able to get the assistance they needed immediately; they also received help in finding more affordable housing. They were able to transition out of Family Assistance and meet their needs on their own.

"Joseph" came to the United States as a refugee from Burundi when he was a child. He grew up, married, and had a family. Over the years, he had faced layoffs and had come to the PRC for help. In addition to food, the PRC provided Joseph with literacy skills, computer training, and job search assistance. Joseph and his wife still use the Food Pantry and the Literacy Program, but they both now have jobs and they are able to make ends meet.

For obvious reasons, no living client can be singled out by name to be highlighted in this history. However, one who has died provided insights into the needs of an individual and the reaction of that individual to the PRC's help. Ralph Luna came to the PRC without a permanent address and no possessions beyond the clothing he was wearing but with a willingness to work for anything he received. Ralph remained at the PRC for five years and became an all-around handyman because he seemed able to fix anything. He saw that parking was a problem and he took on a job that no one else wanted, parking lot director, in the winter. Since the traffic volume in the small parking lot quickly became a problem on mornings of food distribution, a person was needed to stand at the entrance and direct cars to street parking when the parking lot filled. In winter, especially, this was not an easy job, but Ralph persevered and kept order where, before him, there had been congestion and stress on drivers. He found a place that he could sleep at the PRC and it was there he died of an apparent heart at-

tack. His memorial service filled the Hope Presbyterian Church
with 300 staff, volunteers, board members, and clients. His portrait, done after his death by the director of the Art Program, Lesley
Gena, now hangs next to the reception desk in the entry hall. His
stay with his "PRC family" had an impact that continues to inspire.
Ralph became a legend and, in a very real sense, another of those
miracles. Missy Travis, the senior director of programs, spoke at
Ralph's memorial and said of him,

"I don't know if he found us or we found him,
but we needed him and he needed us."

8

The Future

Looking Back and Looking Ahead

THE PAST IS PRELUDE. This old adage certainly applies to the PRC in the second decade of the twenty-first century. The history highlighted in the previous chapters is the basis for its future. Its reputation as a community that welcomes all comers, its continual readiness to expand in order to meet the needs of its clients, and the way it attracts volunteers and donors to share their resources with others are all parts of its past that will shape its future. Some influences on its future, such as the state of the economy and DuPage County's population growth, are beyond the control of its staff and board, but the strategic plan developed by the staff, the board, and Executive Director Kim Perez in 2011 is the direction that the People's Resource Center will take in the immediate future. Kim recognized that the past is prelude in the letter that introduced the plan:

> We have come a long way, indeed. *Last year, People's Resource Center served over 9,000 families, nearly 32,000 individuals.* From our humble beginnings in 1975, handing groceries out to neighbors in need from a small house on Indiana Avenue in Wheaton, we have grown to become a multi-site, multi-service organization serving tens of thousands. All the while, we have remained grounded in

grassroots community support—from volunteers, congregations, service clubs, area businesses, community and family
foundations, generous philanthropic individuals, and clients
themselves who generously give back—to carry out our
"neighbor to neighbor" model of service.

To continue to be a grassroots, volunteer-powered, community-supported organization, it is important that those who join the
"community" as clients, volunteers, staff, board members, or donors understand how the history of the PRC is the basis for the
philosophy that all people who come to the Center are treated with
respect and as equals. This history should provide newcomers with
the realization that neighbors in need can only be helped with the
assistance of many people working together in community and
that listening to those who come in need is the key ingredient in designing new programs.

The immediate future for DuPage County will most probably
involve continued levels of high unemployment and poverty. This
condition will affect more county residents and will place increasing demands on existing programs as well as highlight the need for
new programs. Cuts in federal and state funding have already begun and will continue along with some decreases in private
foundation grants.

Strategic Plan 2011

"Strategic Plan 2011" aims at a two-pronged problem—increased
demand for services and declining funding levels—that the PRC
faces as this history is being written.

Increasing Demands

Increased demand for services has been felt most urgently in
Westmont. The solution is twofold, first, to add more hours to the
time that the food pantry in Westmont is open, and second, to look
for a larger and more permanent facility in Westmont that can handle the growing number of clients seeking services of the ESL, Art,
Computer Training, and Job Assistance programs. This second op-
tion, a lengthy process, is already under way. A more distant
prospect to meet increasing demands is to establish a third PRC location in the northern part of DuPage County. This will require a

detailed feasibility study.

Because of the increased numbers of disabled, elderly, and chronically ill clients, the PRC wants to extend its home food delivery service. For wider access to other services, still more cooperation is needed with existing and new partner organizations that can provide classroom space for art, literacy, and computer program activities. Existing programs will be evaluated professionally so that they will become more effective in delivering their services. These evaluations will benefit staff, volunteers, and board members in their professional development.

Decreasing Revenues

- The PRC will increase advocacy efforts on public policy issues, especially hunger, and on access to educational programs, housing, and job search services as these relate to the client base.
- There will be a need for enhancing public relations efforts in those areas of the county where the PRC is currently not well known.
- Outreach, especially technological, will be upgraded to enhance contact with donors, advocacy groups, local media, and community groups.
- The PRC will seek to work more closely with social service providers to address the gaps in collaboration relating to issues that are considered high priority.
- The PRC will work to establish itself as the local expert on specific advocacy issues for local media and for other community groups.

The main challenge for the future will be to find a balance between maintaining an efficient organization that can serve a rapidly increasing clientele and developing the kinds of new programs that address identified needs at the grassroots, neighbor-to-neighbor level. Volunteers will become an even more critical component in expansion of services as revenues decline.

"Strategic Plan 2011" is the framework for future operations. It is, however, just a framework; it must be built on and filled out. One of the building blocks of the future is partnering and cooperation with other organizations.

Partnering and Cooperation

From the PRC's earliest days, partnering and cooperation with other organizations has been a goal and a reality; the PRC has never been a stand-alone organization. When it comes to raising funds, sharing financial and human resources, delivering services to clients, and making or accepting referrals, the Center has always been cooperative, never competitive. Everyone understands that despite its multi-site and multi-service nature it cannot provide for all its clients' needs. It has in the past relied on governmental and private organizations and it will expand its reliance on both in the future.

In its early years, the PRC was primarily a health care organization. It established the DuPage Community Clinic (DCC) as an independent entity and has continued to refer clients in need of health care to the DCC and to accept clients referred by the clinic. With the expected increase of clients, the PRC will be seeking more partners to whom those with physical, mental, and emotional problems can be referred. But it is not just in the area of health care that referrals are often necessary. At present, more than twenty government and private agencies can and do help clients with housing, education, and jobs. Referral opportunities in these areas will have to be expanded as more neighbors come with multiple needs.

The directors of the empowerment programs, that is, computer training, job assistance, literacy, and art, are likewise continually looking for more classroom space to accommodate clients. At present, there are thirty classrooms for these programs at the College of DuPage, in churches, and in libraries around the county. Not only will more space be needed in the future, but also more volunteers to act as instructors. And these instructors will require more training sessions to prepare them to work with those they will instruct. For all of these programs, future expansion will mean greater complexity because all classroom activities have to be scheduled to accommodate the time restrictions of both student-clients and volunteer-instructors.

Partnering and cooperation with religious congregations has always been a significant part of the PRC tradition. The PRC has support from more than 150 congregations with diverse faith backgrounds. These congregations have helped to raise funds and have provided both long-term and single-event volunteers. They have offered their facilities to be used as classrooms, for meetings, and for volunteer appreciation dinners. Some of the congregations have run food drives for the pantry and a number have made substantial contributions of gifts to "Share the Spirit." Despite the fact that many of these congregations are themselves suffering economically, the PRC depends on their help in the immediate and distant future.

Food providers have been an important source of help since those first boxes of groceries were handed out of the basement window of the house on Indiana Avenue. The Northern Illinois Food Bank has provided low-cost nonperishable food throughout most of the PRC's history. Community gardens have been sources of fresh produce for both of the PRC's locations. Retail food stores have also provided discounts when the pantry ran low. More recently, restaurants have participated in the "Dine Away Hunger"

Mellie Duffy (right) delivering produce
from the V2V's garden to Al White

program, providing cash contributions, and they have raised awareness of hunger in the county. The PRC will continue to rely on all of these sources of cooperation and will seek more such providers as the demand on its own pantry increases.

Two forms of cooperation are directly future oriented. The first is peer organizations. These are groups in which the PRC is linked to other organizations engaged in the same type of work. The Community Hunger Network is a coalition of DuPage area food banks. Melissa Travis, senior director of programs at the PRC, is presently the chair of this network. The Homeless Prevention Committee is a group of organizations and individuals whose aim is to provide housing for those who have lost their homes in the county. The PRC's social worker, Tonya Latson, is the present chair of this group and Executive Director Kim Perez is a board member of the DuPage Federation of Human Service Reform. This is an advocacy group that has as its mission to examine and improve the services available to those in need within the county's boundaries. These three and other groups have been formed to look both at the present and to the future in order to give their member organizations the means to adapt to changing economic, political, and social conditions in the county, state, and nation.

The Center's future-oriented cooperation has been its association with two strong foundation partners, the DuPage Community Foundation and the Community Memorial Foundation. Through their grants these two partners have made major contributions to the work of the PRC. The DuPage Community Foundation manages the PRC's endowment fund and holds donor-advised funds for the Center to request as needed, as well as actively encouraging community-wide philanthropy and volunteerism. The Community Memorial Foundation, in addition to financial support, regularly provides professional development opportunities for the staff and board of directors. These activities are aimed not only at internal development but also at helping all community organizations to work together in the most effective way possible. The future is not an abstract concept and both foundations regularly remind the PRC and their other affiliated organizations of this reality.

The endowment that DuPage Community Foundation manages is due in great part to Linda Cheatham. Linda, as senior director of human resources and finances, was instrumental in getting the board of directors to establish an endowment. She joined the PRC in 1995 when the organization's finances were at an all-time low. She persuaded board members to authorize her to put a small portion of annual contributions into a fund that would be immediately available if a serious financial calamity were to strike. This urgent need for funds surfaced when the PRC purchased its Naperville Road building and found that extensive renovation was required. With yet another building acquisition projected in "Strategic Plan 2011," she feels assured that purchase and renovations could be covered without a serious strain on the daily operating funds needed for clients.

The examples of partnering and cooperation outlined above do not exhaust the list of organizations that have and will be part of the future. As noted earlier, county and township human service offices have referred clients who did not know about the PRC. Local corporations, like CNA, Tellabs, Nicor, Target, Walmart, Sara Lee, and NOW Foods have provided monetary, in-kind, and volunteer aid. Service clubs such as Lions, Rotary, Exchange Club, and Boys and Girls Clubs have been of significant help with food

Cooking demonstration by Mellie Duffy (right)
and Phyllis Smith with produce from V2V's garden

drives and "Share the Spirit." Members of the DuPage Medical Group volunteer on a weekly basis in Westmont. Five chambers of commerce and fifteen banks should be added to this list as must the U.S. Postal Service with its annual food drive. The support from these and many other organizations is more than just part of history. Their support and cooperation represent an affirmation of the PRC's importance to DuPage County and a pledge that in a difficult economy the People's Resource Center will not stand alone.

Models for the Future

Just as the past is prelude, so it is equally true that the future belongs to the young. All at the PRC are well aware of that fact and have begun a pioneering new program aimed at the youth of DuPage County called "Learn and Experience to Advance your Potential" (LEAP). The Winter 2012 edition of the PRC newsletter describes LEAP as a twelve-week intensive work-readiness program for young people aged seventeen to twenty-one. Financial support for the program comes from DuPage Workforce Development, an outreach program of DuPage County that administers the program for the federal Department of Labor. Under the supervision of Elizabeth Higgins, the senior director of empowerment, personnel from job assistance, computer training, literacy, and art programs instruct and tutor students. Also, many of the other departments, pantry, clothes closet, and reception provide work/study assignments for them.

LEAP is one goal of "Strategic Plan 2011"—the expansion of existing programs. LEAP helps young people develop their skills and build on their education and experience to get jobs that will further their careers. In the process, these young people work together and come to understand the importance of a community approach and teamwork in moving into the world of work, and they learn an individual work ethic and the value of diversity in the work environment. They come to rely on each other for support and to see their peers outside the program as friends they can support rather than as competitors. Upon successful completion of the LEAP program, participants receive a certificate.

The PRC in Westmont is yet another model of what can be developed in the future. The rented warehouse-office in Westmont gives the impression of being crowded, and it is just that. Like the

Wheaton location, it is multifunctional, but it is also stretched to its limits. With food distribution in process, job counseling is relegated to a small office and ESL training takes place in the corridor. In the spring, the clothes closet is filled with prom dresses that must be given out quickly because space does not allow for food and clothing distribution to go on at the same time. The southeast area of DuPage County needs the PRC, but the present facility in Westmont is bursting at the seams. Currently, a search is under way for a larger, permanent PRC facility in the southeast area.

The PRC's move to open a food pantry in Westmont's Alliance church in 2002 was a response to the needs of the many clients who had to cross the county for food in Wheaton. Six years later, the church basement was too small and the present location was opened, as a food pantry. The opening of all the other programs, scheduled for 2009, was accelerated because the economic downturn that began in 2008 dramatically increased the number of clients. The 280 families who came to PRC Southeast in Westmont in 2008 were soon joined by more than 500 others so that in 2012, the pantry served 800 families with four food distributions a week.

Hank Anzelone, a Westmont resident, was volunteering as outreach director in his church when he met Mary Ellen in 2001. He became the first of the more than one hundred volunteers to serve at PRC Southeast. He later became a paid staff member. Al White, whose experience with the food pantry dates back to the very early days of the organization, teamed up with Hank and found that the two of them shared the same vision. They wanted not merely to serve those in need, but to address the stigma of poverty by publicizing the existence of the pantry. Thereby they hoped that clients would come for help before they found themselves in dire need. This publicity had the unexpected benefit of getting local residents interested in creative ways to help their neighbors.

A few instances of these creative approaches:

On land provided by churches, volunteers from a group calling itself V2V (Vacant 2 Vegetables), including members of the Hinsdale Garden Club, began planting vegetable gardens to provide the Westmont pantry with fresh vegetables in season. The DuPage Medical Group, which was already sending volunteers each Saturday to staff the pantry's food distribution, began placing bins in its offices throughout the county to collect nonperishable foods. St. Isaac Jogues parish in Hinsdale launched a monthly food drive and a member of the First United Methodist Church in Downers Grove started a one-woman cake sale with all proceeds going to PRC Southeast. This church also holds a monthly food and diaper drive and staffs pantry and intake services twice each month.

Hank and Al, the two Food Pantry staff members, were not merely watching others be creative. Hank started a "food literacy" class that stressed both nutrition in cooking and economical shopping so that clients could make the most of what they received at the pantry. The V2V gardeners came in from the fields and sponsored food literacy cooking demonstrations. Al began collecting pet food from local outlets such as Target, Trader Joe's, and Walmart, which were already donating. Clients with pets were surprised and very grateful for this pantry innovation.

The level of activity one witnesses in Westmont today is a concrete model of what can be done as the PRC expands. By providing a presence in an underserved area of DuPage County, the Center not only reached clients who could not easily come to Wheaton, but it tapped into a pool of dedicated volunteers, over a hundred in the Food Pantry alone. Working with four staff members these volunteers have shown that the PRC can replicate itself. Westmont has found the resources and has made clients welcome. Because it has fit so well into the community, the PRC now looks forward to a more spacious facility to provide even better service for those who come for help. Identifying needs and working to create solutions has been and will continue to be the founding principle of the PRC. In other areas in DuPage County needs have already been identified but have not yet been addressed. The task now is to learn from this Westmont model and craft solutions for the future.

Two international connections also serve as models for the PRC's future. The first involved a group of visitors from Germany. In 1997, a group of five social workers from Caritas, the German equivalent of Catholic Charities, spent a day helping out in the Food Pantry and the Clothes Closet. Sponsored by a Bosch Foundation grant this visit aimed to give the social workers an opportunity to observe American not-for-profit organizations and to interact with staff and volunteers. They wanted to learn about the administration and fund-raising efforts of these private organizations, because in Germany many social services are provided by the government, and voluntary agencies and services are not common. Some of their comments illustrate how much they appreciated learning how a small group of private citizens can address the needs of their neighbors.

> I learned that you tackle a problem even if your means are limited. In the United States the private social sector is a good complement to the government sector. It is based on citizens' initiatives. In Germany, I see a lack of passion with which the Americans carry out their engagement with others.

While they intended to take new ideas home with them, they also suggested new possibilities for the PRC. When they returned to Germany, they rented a four-story building that now houses a clothes closet and a furniture repair and resale shop. Both give employment to seamstresses and carpenters who repair donated items that are then sold at discounted prices. In the process they train apprentices in each field.

The second international connection is the Middle East Partnership Initiative (MEPI). Benedictine University in Lisle receives yearly grants from the Department of State to bring students from high schools and colleges in the Middle East to its campus. The goal of the program is to foster improved understanding of culture, attitudes, and behaviors between the visitors and the Americans they meet.

As one of their outreach activities, the MEPI students visited the PRC for the past two years. They spent a day helping out in the Food Pantry and the Clothes Closet and they discussed with staff and volunteers their own cultures and the needs the Center is addressing. Their first reaction was disbelief that such poverty amidst the obvious wealth of DuPage County caused so many people to wait in line to get food and other services.

Advocacy

Advocacy is another future-oriented activity that is not new to the organization and is closely connected to partnering and cooperation. From the beginning, Dorothy was tireless in presenting to political and religious leaders in DuPage County the fact that, contrary to all assumptions, there were poor people living in their midst. That message must still be conveyed to some leaders but the message has now expanded to "How can we meet the needs of the poor among us?" Through the years, under the directorship of Mary Ellen, advocacy was continued and significantly expanded. Mary Ellen and both staff and volunteers visited county, state, and national leaders to find ways to get the message across. Kim began early in her tenure as executive director to meet present political, religious, and business leaders with the same message because memories can be short and the content of the message must always be kept fresh in the minds of those who continually face a wide variety of issues. All at the PRC know that the future will require even more intensive advocacy. At the same time, however, the political, religious, and economic neutrality that has served the Center so well in the past must be maintained.

Strategic planning and cooperation and advocacy are absolutely essential for an organization that has grown to the present size of the PRC. How these activities translate into everyday services always comes down to the way in which volunteers and staff members meet their neighbors. A PRC volunteer working in the food pantry on one particularly busy day summed up the short- and long-term outlook for the organization with one terse sentence:
"Look, the future happens every day
when we open our doors."

Epilogue

THE RICH HISTORY OF THE PEOPLE'S RESOURCE CENTER is the foundation on which this organization rests today. This history continues to teach, inform, and inspire the actions and decisions made all these years after Dorothy and Tom met. The PRC remains a place where neighbors in need seek out help, hope, and opportunity. It is also a place where neighbors come to *provide* that help, hope, and opportunity. It is in these acts of both receiving and giving that the PRC has become and remains more than a place, but a community.

When I was being recruited as executive director, I had the opportunity to meet and get to know many people involved with the People's Resource Center. During a lunch meeting with a few members of the board of directors, two of whom also happened to be original members of REC—Bob Russo and Warren Roth—I was first introduced to the notion of the PRC being a community. Warren was passionate about making sure that I understood how this sense of community was at the center of the PRC and everything that has been accomplished through this organization. He was also intent on gauging my commitment to ensuring that this would be carried forward if I were to become the next executive director. In fact, this focus on community has been one of my beacons and guiding principles during the first two years of my leadership at the PRC.

It is my belief that everything about the People's Resource Center relates to the power of community. We are proud that—thanks to the tireless volunteerism of our team of more than 1,600 volunteers—we are a community-powered organization.

(*Note:* At the time this book was written in 2011, volunteers numbered 1,300. By August 2012 the number had risen to 1,600.)

And we remain a community-supported organization, with more than half of our annual revenue coming from individuals in the community, and another significant portion coming from local organizations, churches, and civic groups. And, most importantly, all of our programs and services are available to our DuPage County community members who are struggling to make ends meet.

Simply walking through the doors at the PRC brings to life this sense of community. If you haven't yet had the chance to do so, please come visit us. Many of our visitors have shared that they are struck by the warm welcome they received, regardless of their reason for visiting. Such experiences have been shared by clients, volunteers, employees, and countless other visitors. It simply doesn't matter what language you speak, the country from which you originate, the political views that you maintain, your religious beliefs, or even your age or gender. The diversity of the PRC community provides strength for what we accomplish together and is a fundamental part of the amazing mosaic that makes up the People's Resource Center.

While times have changed since Dorothy, Tom, and the members of REC began providing food and other supports out of that basement window on Indiana Avenue, much has also remained the same. In fact, the need in DuPage County has arguably never been greater. The local poverty rate is the highest it has ever been. Unemployment remains high. The cost of living in DuPage County is higher than in neighboring counties, and costs continue to rise. Last year, more than 32,000 individuals—more than 9,300 households—received services from the People's Resource Center. A snapshot of how the PRC community reached out to those neighbors in need over the past year shows:

- More than 2.4 million pounds of food were distributed by our two food pantries.
- The PRC provided 7,971 families with 37,202 grocery carts filled with a week's worth of nutritious food, including fresh produce, frozen meats, and bread.
- 1,733 households selected gently used, seasonally appro-

priate clothing for their families.
- 220 families received financial assistance to regain housing stability.
- 728 families were connected to additional social services including SNAP (food stamps), emergency financial assistance, and health care.
- 595 adults enrolled in English as a Second Language classes, studied for GED and citizenship exams, or worked with tutors to achieve their learning goals.
- 134 children boosted their academic skills through the PRC's hands-on Summer Science program.
- 1,100 adults registered for computer classes.
- 751 families received free, refurbished computers for their homes.
- 843 families received free repairs and maintenance for their home computers.
- 164 people found jobs with guidance from PRC job mentors.
- 381 individuals received job assistance services.
- 221 adults and 410 children developed their self-esteem and creativity through PRC art programs.

As the community need continues to grow, the community response must keep pace. The team of volunteers must continue to grow and cash and in-kind support must continue to increase so that we have the resources to meet the needs of our neighbors. The People's Resource Center has been demonstrated through all these years as a powerful community response to critical community problems. I hope that you have been inspired by all that you've read and will share the story of the People's Resource Center with those around you. As the early REC members so clearly understood, as individuals we *can* make a difference that becomes even stronger and more impactful when we join together to take action as a community.

Miracles Relied Upon documents and preserves the many events that have brought the People's Resource Center to 2012. The authors of this book, Margaret and Warren Roth, have been part of the PRC community since the very beginning. Their writing of this book was done in a volunteer capacity to preserve the rich history of this organization. I, along with the board of directors of the People's Resource Center, could not be more grateful for their generosity.

Finally, to all of you who have been a part of the People's Resource Center community in some way, thank you. Thank you for all you do every day to help our neighbors in need. So many lives have been improved. So many needs have been met. So many hearts

Kim Perez

have been touched. None of this would have been possible without the help of thousands of individuals, countless hours of dedicated time, and immeasurable generosity. I am honored to serve the People's Resource Center and to be a member of this community. Thank you for making hope and opportunity a reality for everyone who walks through our doors.

Kim Perez, Executive Director
People's Resource Center
August 2012

To make a donation, become a volunteer, or learn more
about People's Resource Center, please visit our website:
www.peoplesrc.org.